Less Noise, More Soul

LESS

NOISE

MORE

SOUL

THE SEARCH FOR BALANCE IN THE ART, TECHNOLOGY, AND COMMERCE OF MUSIC

edited by DAVID FLITNER

Hal Leonard Books
An Imprint of Hal Leonard Corporation

Acknowledgments

This book began as a commentary piece in *Billboard* magazine, and were it not for Ken Schlager and Sarah Han, formerly of that publication, it might never have moved beyond a condition of gestation. The book's title is adapted from that original article, and I am grateful to *Billboard* and to Louis Hau for its use.

Each of the writers in the collection has made a contribution based on a single premise: a profound passion for music at its best. My gratitude to them for their sharing of experience and wisdom cannot be overstated. Initiation of the project was aided immeasurably by the enthusiasm of Will Ackerman, Rob Reinhart, and especially Bob Ludwig, an individual respected by all and whose dedication to excellence is exceeded only by his generosity.

Special thanks to John Cerullo, Bernadette Malavarca, Iris Bass, and Jaime Nelson of Hal Leonard Performing Arts Publishing Group.

Thank you to my parents, David and Mariam Flitner, for their enduring supportiveness.

And to my wife, Cara, my heartfelt thanks for your patience, unfailing assistance, and belief.

few? Is the machinery the problem? Has the pool of worthy composers dried up? Have record labels and radio largely squashed the vitality out of what seems available?

In May 2005, the professional recording magazine *Mix* replaced its normal cover photo of a sophisticated recording facility with a loud orange background and slapdash lettering spelling out a single question: Who Cares About Quality? The new era has brought possibility, promise, and unprecedented opportunities for the democratization of creativity and its distribution without the need for major labels—and permitted mediocrity to sparkle and shimmer as if it represented hard work and talent. Technology is available as a partner in production, becoming an extension of an organic process of expression, even as it is complicit in the strangling compression of audio quality solely to facilitate portability and convenience for consumers who seem unaware of—or unconcerned with—what has been sacrificed. Indeed, software is touted that purports to deconstruct parameters of a piece of music and predict the likelihood of its being a hit before anyone in the public has heard it. Perhaps the only clear conclusion to be reached is that of engineer Steve Albini, who has said the current milieu is one in which "everybody is equally confused."

Music and technology have been working out their relationship for a long time, from early pianos which could not accommodate the full range of composers' notes, to Bob Dylan's use of the electric guitar for folk music, to the introduction of a box for the correction of errant—yet human—vocal pitch. It's all technology, from plectrum to

Pro Tools. That which is embraced as an innovative answer by some is seen as apostasy by others. This may reflect any number of individual, esthetic, and cultural factors, from a new generational sensibility for which melody and harmony do not resonate meaningfully, to assumed premises regarding the very concept of progress to, more mundanely, a simple lack of imagination.

The contributors to this volume, many of them award winners, bring a true wealth of experience and insight to a parsing of the new paradigm and its variegated yet interrelated elements. Their backgrounds encompass composition, performance, engineering, production, record labels, broadcasting, and education. Some of their essays display the characteristics of a rousing op-ed piece, others the erudition of a considered treatise, others the sheer vitality of stream of consciousness vamping, and some have the feel of good conversation; exactly what we should expect when the subject is music, the creative form which energizes and soothes, rhapsodizes and annoys— the essential artistic soundtrack of the human journey.

The opinions voiced are varied and unfiltered. Yet they share a common purpose of starting the process of asking more honest questions about the ways in which good music comes into being and how it can maintain its integrity from the composer's heart to the listener's ear. The overall perspective is neither that of the "if it's new, it's better" advocate nor that of the Luddite. Consensus is sought only as a product of open inquiry. And honest divergence of outlook may be taken as fully reflective of Bob Dylan's recollection in "Tangled Up in Blue": "We always did feel the same/We just saw it from a different point of view."

On February 9, 1964, a revolution was set in motion. Understandably, British readers may be forgiven for objecting that said process was already well underway, but, arguably, the first appearance of the Beatles on the *Ed Sullivan Show* in the United States marked the signal point of departure for what the late, brilliant (and British) writer Ian MacDonald called a "revolution in the head" of Western, and even world, culture. Very little has been the same since. Popular music rapidly became something surpassingly more than a genial backdrop, transforming itself inextricably into a fundamental component of an explosive process of change, the ramifications of which continue to resonate and consternate now into a new millennium. Music matters. And the means of its gestation and birth are of relevance far beyond the studio.

Writer and activist Rick Bass has said, "Two things—any two things, with differences between them, whether small or great, will always be carving at one another, until some change satisfactory to the universe occurs." It is to be hoped that this creative interplay will find its way to characterizing the making of music, with increasingly sophisticated tools, by very human beings. For if, in the words of pianist and scholar Charles Rosen, music is a "basic human need," then there is an aesthetic—if not moral—obligation to address this precarious and delicate issue of balance in an area of culture that touches so many so profoundly.

A Boomer's Lament on the Devaluation of Music

by LYDIA HUTCHINSON

I lost my iPod last week, and, quite honestly, I'm shocked at how little it mattered to me. Other than the cost of the equipment itself, it held no real value—a fact unknown to me until it was gone, left in the backseat of a Chicago cab to blow around the Windy City. And I find my lack of grief over losing hundreds of songs organized into perfect playlists, well . . . grief-worthy.

While I was growing up, music was the thing that mattered *most*. Saving my allowance, riding my bike to the TG&Y dollar store on Saturday, flipping through record bins, spreading my crumpled babysitting money on the counter and then biking home with a new treasure under my arm were part of the whole experience. Once home I'd go into my room, close the door, and stretch out on the green shag carpet for that exciting first listen. Songs became imprinted in my mind by their order on each side of the album, memorized with the inevitable pops and scratches that became etched in certain places. In fact, those scratches are what made them personal, adding a value that was beyond measure.

I knew every detail of the photos on the sleeve, memorized the lyrics and had my own game of trivia with the producers, musicians, and songwriters whose credits appeared on each album—just in case there was a chance to show off that knowledge during a high-school dance. (Actually, opportunities for such trivia abounded near the punch bowl where the wallflowers and nerds congregated.) We called it "fondling the vinyl."

And there was the aspect of our social life—before becoming mall rats or hanging out in Mr. Gatti's parking lots—where we'd sit around with a friend and listen to an entire album: Fleetwood Mac's *Rumours*, Heart's *Dreamboat Annie*, Carole King's *Tapestry*, Billy Joel's *The Stranger*, Michael Jackson's *Thriller*—all perfect records with no filler songs. Even KC and the Sunshine Band's self-titled disco masterpiece had us spinning around our rooms, perfecting line-dancing skills, and getting our recommended daily allowance of exercise (just another benefit music provided).

I guess that's what frustrates me about the digitization of music: It's ideal for portability, accessibility, and one-off songs. But what's missing is the *experience* of music. The visuals, the sequence of songs, the sonic quality, the community aspect of listening, and the tangible object that you treasure and which can bring back a lifetime of memories.

I also realize these lamentations come from the tragic heart of a baby boomer. I'm one of around 78 millions kids of Depression-era parents, born at the tail end of an eighteen-year cultural generation. We were defined on the front end by the civil rights movement and the Vietnam War, and on the back end by Watergate and the television show *thirtysomething*. In other words, my generation consists of free-spirited cynics who trust the government about as far as we can throw it.

Through it all, however, music was our generational identity. Rock and roll, much to our delight, drove our parents crazy. The Beatles turned our world upside down. Portable transistor radios provided the freedom to listen to whatever we wanted, whenever we wanted. We gave birth to everything from Motown to punk to disco. And music festivals touting beaded love, freedom from authority, and psychedelic head trips were our muddy mark. Music, in all its forms, was a shared experience that united us, so it's understandable that we're not dealing well with all the changes going on. As a matter of fact, I'd say we're completely undone.

In our graying and oft-addled heads, of course, music was what we gave the world, so we can't help feeling protective of it these days. How we listened to it, discovered it, shared it, and collected it provided a sense of pride and purpose.

And the mere thought of something as valuable as music becoming a disposable commodity is nothing short of devastating to us. We coveted albums and built shelves to display them like they were fine art. And we felt like we had access to every song that was made and never feared missing out on something great; there were a finite number of avenues to discover music, and that gave us a sense of control.

Of course that illusion of control is long gone, which might explain why we and our enormous egos are so tipped over. Pristine recordings are now condensed MP3s? Extravagant studios reserved for the elite are now set up in homes so anyone can make a record? Songs are downloadable and oftentimes free? Cover art and packaging are becoming obsolete? People are walking around with little plugs in their ears, listening to thousands of songs stored on a player the size of my thumb? Or on a cell phone, for crying out loud? And these warp-speed changes for a group who nearly needed therapy after being asked to go from manually placing a needle onto a vinyl disc to pushing buttons that read Fast Forward, Rewind, Play, or Stop has piled insult on top of injury.

So here sits my entire generation. A cumulative "bitter, party of one" with a table waiting.

Luckily, my Depression-era mother is far more embracing of change than her boomer daughter. As I was dragging her down some nostalgic road trip recently, pining away for the good old days while nobly sipping on a glass of red wine, she just laughed and said, "Honey, remember, someone will be referring to *this* as the good old days before long. So go on and find the positives and, for once in your life, enjoy it while you're in the middle of it." I hate it when she's right.

So I started thinking about how incredible this time really is, and how it must feel to the younger generations who are, indeed, taking technology to places we'd never dreamed. And from that perspective, the limitless possibilities of discovering music today are thrilling. The playing field, even though it's incredibly crowded, is completely level now, and there are hundreds of ways to stumble upon great songs—music that doesn't need money and major label support to reach our ears.

And the reality is that this fast-paced digital highway of music is the product of independent spirits who have built their own businesses, based on their own rules. They're road warriors who have logged tens of thousands of miles in their beat-up vehicles to build their fan base and get their music out into the world. And they're creative thinkers who can switch lanes to create new opportunities, while the major labels are gasping for air, lumbering behind, and chasing yesterday's trend. We're in the middle of a revolution with the independents leading the way—and that's something all generations can support.

I was talking recently with a group of industry friends, all of us about the same age except for a wonderfully creative hip-hop artist whom I adore for his seemingly unlimited patience with us. As we were grousing about the industry, the perils of downloading, the lack of sonic quality in today's recordings, and how great music used to be, he just smiled and basically told us the boat's already sailed, and it would be much more productive if we just figured out how to get onboard and enjoy all it had to offer. Again, I hate it when someone else is right.

So, I'm almost ready to pack my bags, get on the boat, and be excited about all the ways we have to discover and enjoy music now. And if those who have already fearlessly set sail will indulge me and my generation during our inevitable walks down memory lane, we'd really appreciate it. Change is hard, but we've been through enough to know it's inevitable. And once we quit kicking and screaming, I'm certain we'll be able to see the beauty in it. And knowing us, we'll take credit for that, too.

The Qualities of Feeling, Time, and Illogic

by RICK CLARK

Ever since I was a kid, I've been tremendously fascinated with the idea of recorded sound. When I was in the third grade I remember being at a friend's house and dying to get this little basic reel-to-reel recorder I saw in a catalog. This took place during the middle '60s. I just remember wanting this machine so badly, but the idea of actually owning something like that seemed so out of my reach. My friend had a little reel-to-reel recorder, so I was able to fantasize and glean something from the experience vicariously. Even back then it wasn't so much the idea of capturing sound in a documentary way that engaged my imagination, as much as it was the idea of manipulating those sounds into something that excited me in the way my favorite records captured my heart.

My first recording device was a Concord cassette recorder that I got for Christmas in the late '60s. By then, I was making noise on a variety of instruments and was beginning to play in a band. I actually have a stereo recording of my very first gig, which was in 1969. It was recorded on one of the early Panasonic stereo cassette recorders. I'm so glad I still have that tape, so I can listen to how we massacred Pink Floyd, early Steve Miller band, Blodwyn Pig, Led Zeppelin, Spencer Davis, and Booker T. and the MGs. We even did an "original" song, which was a terribly sloppy and over-wrought twelve-bar English blues rock number called "Hey Baby."

I had only played bass guitar for a few months when I did my first recording session in a proper studio, which was called Block Six. We were recording some songs to perform on a local television show called *Talent Party*, which was hosted by WHBQ-AM deejay George Klein, who was a member of Elvis's Memphis Mafia—the first man I ever met who wore a load of makeup. I distinctly remember the studio owner and engineer, Larry Rogers, telling me that I was supposed to play the bass with a pick instead of with my fingers. For better or worse, I guess you can say that was the first time I was produced.

There really wasn't a music outlet for me in school for learning recording or gleaning tips on how to be a "rock god." I played bass drum and glockenspiel in the ROTC band and ended up skipping the last half of high school, playing my music and recording it, poring over my favorite records and working at the local record store. When I wasn't doing that, I was often hanging out and playing my guitar or drawing pictures up on the railroad trestles over the Mississippi River, something I did hundreds and hundreds of times.

All in all, I'm really grateful that I grew up in Memphis, Tennessee, during the '50s and '60s and '70s, because there was such an abundance of incredible music like Sun Records (Elvis, Charlie Rich, Jerry Lee Lewis, Carl Perkins, Howlin' Wolf, Johnny Cash, Roy Orbison), Stax (Otis Redding, Sam & Dave, Rufus and Carla Thomas), Hi Records (Al Green, Ann Peebles, Otis Clay), and many others. I didn't really understand just how special it was until I was older and many of the great local record labels had collapsed. I thought every town was as blessed as Memphis or, for that matter, the regional triangle of Memphis, Nashville, and Muscle Shoals, Alabama.

By the middle '70s, I was actively part of a small but passionate Anglophile rock pop scene, and when we weren't learning things by trial and error in one of the local studios, we were laying down sounds on my TEAC 3340 four-track recorder. One of the studios where we learned the ropes was a place called Shoe Recording, owned by Warren Wagner and Wayne Crook. They were great guys who gave us loads of hours to experiment and lay down anything that came into our head. What they offered was a true gift. In the beginning, their recording console was a totally homemade affair that looked like an old vehicle gas tank full of wires, with faders and knobs cut into the side of the metal. The whole thing rested on two metal folding chairs. Shoe started off with eight tracks and then went to sixteen tracks and we mixed to a two-track Studer.

At the time, Ardent Recording was (and is) Memphis's finest state-of-the-art studio. It embodied the dream destination for any artist or rock band that ever wanted to make a serious recording. To record at Ardent was to have arrived, so to speak. It had all the greatest gear and the best engineers, and the vibe in every room made you feel like you were going to do great work. Of course, being in a place like that also made you feel like the clock wasn't your friend. Unless you were block-booking a month, it was easy to feel the pressure of "time is money."

That said, recording studios like Ardent were a far-off dream for most people. It made me long for the day when recording could be done with great facility, offering seemingly endless creative possibilities, in a manner that most people could reasonably afford. Oddly enough, by the time digital recording on computers began making their mark in every home or project studio, I found myself hating the way most of those in-the-box recordings sounded. I had become very acclimated to the sound of music captured by really good engineers using great mics and outboard tools in beautifully designed recording spaces. As it turned out, the very thing I would have loved to have had as a kid—something like GarageBand on a laptop—I postponed embracing for years. These days, there's almost no excuse for not throwing yourself into the wonders of learning how to record sound and create something meaningful out of it. Most creatively inclined people in music seem to feel that way. And that's good. But now we have a double-edged sword: lots and lots

transistorized plastic AM radios in our backyard or by the community pool.

When I listened to some of the great rock and soul records, they had astonishing impact, even if they used a lot of compression (enhanced, ironically, by the limitations of the medium on which they were recorded). I'm certainly not one to totally fixate about the "good old days," because there is good music being made right now. Some of it is quite good, while there's also a load of uninteresting stuff. But it's all out there for a reason.

Recently, I've heard more of a return to dynamic recording, almost exclusively from indie sources. An increasing number of artists, many of them younger, have checked out older recordings and realized, as they listened to a John Coltrane album or a Beatles album, that those classic recordings amply had all the sonic elements of bass, treble, and midrange. The sound was full-bodied and there was a soundstage with plenty of air in it to provide dimensionality. A number of these new younger artists, engineers, producers, and music listeners have astutely begun wondering how those records achieved that sensibility. They have many of the same essential tools, and they even have software that gives them greater facility and ease of use. But they are also aware that many of their recordings lack something that is hard to articulate: that illogical, bigger-than-the-parts, organic ebb and flow that made classic records truly special.

What I believe many creative people desire when writing, performing, and producing music, is to create an experience that is so rewarding that it can stand up to many repeated listenings: in other words, truly durable music.

For a number of years now, we've been inundated with music that is largely devoid of dynamics, and I believe this has made even the most potentially durable recordings fatiguing to experience past more than just a few listens. I personally find the spiritual root of this approach to recording, mixing, producing, and mastering to be fear-based and even cynical, because I think it is mistrustful of the emotional intelligence of the listener. The need to have the loudest recording on the block doesn't trust the intrinsic power found in the material, the performance, and the production of the recording.

Earlier recordings were often a throbbing illogical mess that directed you to key almost uncontrollable moments, depending on whatever was loudest in the signal path. The result certainly wasn't a documentary representation of the actual performance, but an exaggeration or amplification of the elemental experience that was a combination of what happened performance-wise on the studio floor, the way it was engineered, and the way the producer or mixer behind the console emotionally reacted to what was coming out of the speakers. If it was merely a documentary representation of what happened out on the floor, it wouldn't convey many of the visceral elements that informed the excitement behind a performance—largely due to the absence of visual stimulation and other energetic elements experienced during a live event.

This is not entirely dependent upon heavy application of technology or comparisons with what everyone else is doing.

You only listen to one record at a time. Of course, this kind of perspective might be debatable for some in the "Ritalin media" and the culture at large. We live in a time of short attention spans. But I do think that great movies, great art, and great music reached peaks and depths that were transcendent largely as a result of moments that contained lulls or silence, moments to breathe and savor. Whenever everything's constantly going *so* fast, for some of the people that are totally in that flow, it provides its own highs. But if you're always in that state, I wonder where you find the time to have the silence that helps take all those elements and clay and form them into something that is truly rich, providing meaningful depth.

When I was producing Adler and Hearne's *To The Heart* a couple of summers ago, it was very important to me to express that we needed to make a record that could be fearlessly quiet. I wanted it to have enough air in it, when you were hearing the music, that it would engage you because it was dynamically taking you places, that there were spaces for you to inhale and exhale. You could be *in* the music. In the mix I tried manually to nuance the dynamics to make sure that certain points were heard, to carry you to another point. For mastering we went to Andrew Mendelson, a very versatile and sensitive engineer, at Georgetown Mastering. He barely touched the work. It was important to try to protect the performances and those natural dynamics, to make the music durable.

I feel very strongly that there are certain things in music and art toward which people gravitate personally. Everyone has a different read on what touches him or her, of course. In my own case, I seem to be drawn toward music where I feel there is something at risk of being lost, something at stake. It could be a moment where you felt as if a train wreck were about to happen. It could be a moment where you knew, in no uncertain terms, that something occurred that was larger than all of the elements. It could be an incredibly slick, über-produced, L.A.–Quincy Jones thing or it could be the Sex Pistols. It doesn't matter to me. But if I feel like something happened that I couldn't possibly have predicted and controlled, it's that moment.

When I sense that there was something put on the line, where there was risk of losing control, it reminds me of my mortality and of why life is so priceless and precious. It can come in the form of any kind of music. When it happens it makes me glad that I'm alive. Even if it's a song that makes me terribly sad or melancholy, it turns up the colors in my existence, and I find myself grateful. Or it might be one of the songs that makes you just want to drive fast and feel like you're impregnable, untouchable. Those are the things I look for. And in those moments, when I feel them, I know I have a durable listening experience on my hands.

The song might not be a great song. The singer might not be a great singer. The production might actually suck. But if something happens, it's almost always *in spite* of the people involved. Because I think there's something divine. I'm not a religious person, per se. But art, and music particularly, is a path or element for tapping into something that, when it works, our ego can't control.

From my point of view, you can pretty safely say that art happens in spite of artists. Something which is especially disheartening is that when I hear music that is so vitally compressed and limited, what I hear is fear. And what I hear is cynicism. I hear ego, fear-driven ego. It's the thing that makes rock not rock any more, the thing that makes what might be truly affecting, poignant moments become sappy and preachy. It's when the artist destroys the art because the ego needs to edit and control things to death. When you have mixes and productions that are overcompressed and limited, in a way that you often hear in the "loudness wars," what you are experiencing is fear and cynicism and a mistrust that the audience's emotional intelligence isn't capable of handling it in its pure expression. The thing that happens then is that rock no longer rocks, it sounds desperate. When rock *rocks*, there's no desperation. Even if the essence of a song is angry or desperate or edgy, that is a function of the source of creative moment. But when it is captured and chewed up and spit out in a way that over-amplifies that essence, in bold markers, it's like bludgeoning the listener. It's like standing under a perfectly blue sky, and my beating you with a sign saying: "THE SKY IS BEAUTIFULLY BLUE!"

To which you might reply, "I can't see the sky because you're hitting me with a damn sign!"

"Well, I have to *hit* you so that you can see the sky! That's the way it is! What do you mean, you're screaming, 'Ouch'? Don't you want to experience the sky?!"

"No, I want to turn the radio off and walk away."

One of the things particularly frustrating about music that's too thought out is the tendency to tidy up and control things to a point that artists, producers, and engineers are analyzing instead of feeling. Their analytical processes are getting in the way of their emotional receptors. I think if you truly are allowing yourself to experience, the moment you need to decide whether something needs to be looked at differently is the moment when you suddenly are aware that you've been listening for three minutes and twenty-two seconds and the work has not caught your interest and engaged you any longer. Then you must ask, "Is this serving a place for me? Does it set me up for the next ride on the roller coaster? Or is this the place where everyone lost—and if I don't call it for what it is, then I'm just being lazy?" Generally, if there's something that's moving along and I'm actually feeling it, then I should trust that.

When I'm producing, I make sure that I protect things from becoming too linear because that's one of the things that makes a lot of music end up being flat, just as much as people tuning things too much, or playing to a click track so much that there's no groove. You need to protect the ebb and flow of the creative moment. And particularly, when you're dealing with things that are run through all kinds of synthesizers, you've got to do things to disengage the predictability of the sequences and sounds. No matter how good they are, you've got to do things that disarm them. Because predictability will rob you of any potential emotional moment, if you're not paying attention. If you're using something trancelike or hypnotic and predictable to set up something that will be a surprise, you need to make sure that you're really paying attention to how you're feeling so you can know how to let the emotional payoff unfold.

The thing that's ruined more music is too much thinking. And you can *hear* the thinking. That's the "art in spite of artists" thing. What's really sad in rock and roll, with these incredibly smashed-to-the-ceiling kind of loud recordings, is that the level of fear and cynicism has fueled overthinking to the point where it has become not overthinking anymore; it's become second nature. Which is terrifying. It's no longer a process; rather, "Well, this is how you do it." Then you go into a studio and you see these young engineers with their rigs. They automatically slap the approach du jour on your work because it makes it sound like "what it's supposed to sound like," in their mind, because it's what they hear. In a way, what they're doing is prechewing the music as opposed to giving it a chance to reveal itself. That's when it becomes tragic.

In the '80s, when you would go into a session, the first thing the engineer would do was gate the drums. Or he'd want to gate a horn section and remove the breathing from the horn stabs. But often with the horn players, the way they breathe, before the stab, is like a rhythmic grace note. Why would you take that out? If you take the breath, the breathing out of the musical track, aren't you taking the life out of it? There are times when it's appropriate to remove things. But when it becomes reflexive, you're being a follower rather than a creator. And if you're only a follower, you're not really adding anything to the dialogue. You're just eating up everyone's time.

More facility can actually encourage lazy behavior. It's not the fact that you have the facility. It's the fact that human nature sort of gleefully goes down the path of entropy. And not even realizing that it *is*! It's "fixed" but it's not better. If you don't have to apply yourself emotionally in the moment, and you can just "fix it," then you're creating a musical document that will never *be* in the moment.

When you're creating music, it's still about what comes out of your heart and your fingers and your mouth and your feet. No amount of facility can compensate, ultimately, for an inability to skillfully and honestly use the sources from your heart and your hands and your mouth and your feet! It still comes from there. If you just switch on a button and it plays a groovy little sequence over and over again, that's all cool and well, to a point. But it's still a good thing to add a surprise or a nonlinear element, something human, to provide contrast to the uniformity.

Rock is a language: the guitar, bass, drums, maybe keyboards. That language and the twelve-tone scale have been explored ad infinitum. I've heard a lot of people say, "Young bands, they just don't know how to play like bands any more. They don't know how to play a pocket like a classic great band." That's an excessive generalization. The truth is that there are vastly more opportunities for a lot more people to make a lot more music.

Just the sheer volume of newly released music probably makes it seem like there are more people who can't play! But there are plenty of up-and-coming people who are exceptional musicians. It must be remembered that not every band—the Rolling Stones, for example—started out as incredibly skilled musicians. This was a band that eventually recorded "Satisfaction"! It isn't necessary to be the most technically gifted musician to make cool music, especially if you are comfortable and in touch with your own pricelessness enough to throw it away.

There are many cases of bands and musicians who started out making great music, who could barely play one string on a guitar; and the better they got, the more boring their music became. From my point of view, Janis Joplin's original band, Big Brother and the Holding Company, demonstrated this memorably. Her subsequent solo work on *Pearl* never nailed me like listening to "Ball and Chain," "Combination of the Two," "Summertime," or "Piece of My Heart," from Big Brother and the Holding Company's masterful *Cheap Thrills*. She obviously was the center of the stage. But in *Cheap Thrills*, there were those monstrously great psychedelic guitar players that could just play their asses off and a rhythm section that was hanging on for dear life. They were not technically accomplished musicians but they embodied, in that record, that element of risk of something being lost. When you listen to the guitar lead on "Combination of the Two" or "Summertime," you're almost hanging on every note as he's feeling his way to, "What in the world is my next note gonna be?!" You can *feel* that creative unfolding! And that's golden!

The things that helped create the climate for Sun Records, Stax, Motown, Hi, and the San Francisco sound, were a once-in-a-millennium confluence of young populist art in an era of incredible social and political upheaval. Rock and roll, and soul music, happened at a time when there was no Internet; there wasn't even FM radio, there were no cell phones, and there were no color TVs during some of that. Terrestrial AM radio was driven by charts, payola, DJs, and ads. And word of mouth. You'd be at Walgreens and see a Kinks album. There was no file sharing. You bought the record or heard it at a friend's house. And until the late '60s you didn't have a recorder unless you had your father's reel-to-reel. People who complain about MP3s now seem to forget that a lot of us grew up listening to transistor radios, which sounded as bad or worse in some ways. It's not that things were "better" back then. But it was different.

Back then, the recording studios and radio stations used compressors. They smashed everything to bits, but they did it in an incredibly nonlinear way. Whether you're doing a bluegrass record or a folk album, or even a symphony or a jazz thing, it's pretty documentary for the most part. But rock and roll, and a lot of pop music, were as much producers' and engineers' mediums as they were anything. So, when you had a George Martin record or a Mickey Most production, like the Animals or Herman's Hermits or Donovan, or something from Motown or Phil Spector, there was a distinction because, as someone once said, there are recordings and then there are Records. Again, a record wasn't concerned about being a documentary representation of the band. It was about capturing a three-minute slice of something which was a composite of nonprofessional and professional musicians, in a studio, with varying degrees of ineptness or knowledge, and then blowing it onto a slab of vinyl. So, when I listen to "You've Lost That Lovin' Feeling" or "Strawberry Fields Forever," or "Talk Talk" by the Music Machine or "Hurdy Gurdy Man" by Donovan, I know I'm not listening to what it really sounded like. Rather, I'm hearing a creation.

One of the things that I liked about those records, which makes some audiophiles cringe (and probably made people complain even back then), can be heard on the Animals' recording of "Inside Looking Out." When the bass kicks in and Eric Burden is singing, suddenly the drums disappear. And then it's all bass guitar. Then, when the guitar starts playing a line, suddenly everything else ducks down and the guitar is louder than hell. Or you could hear this on a Hendrix record. Whatever was the loudest thing in the signal path sort of won the contest at that second. I liked it because it made everything so nonlinear. It almost said, "Okay, here I am. Okay, I'm gone. Here's the drum. Okay, now it's the singer." The way things were mixed and mastered back then, the compressor/limiter was like the spoon in a stew: stirring the mix around, pulling up the potatoes at one moment, and pulling up the tomatoes over here, and then it's the black-eyed peas' moment. But it was always changing and always saying, "Okay, listen to this moment." Obviously, that's an effect. But especially at the height of the '60s and '70s, it was really appealing when it was used not as a loudness device, but as a creative device.

Try this: turn on the car radio and pick a rock station at random. Chances are that you'll hear some kind of fill-in-the-blank, this decade kind of big rock tune, all screaming and earnest. They're hitting you with their "the-sky-is-blue song." And when the chorus comes in, it doesn't get any louder. You can alter the volume on the station to any level, and the voice, no matter whether it's screaming at you or it's being thoughtful, will remain at exactly the same level. The only thing that *does* happen is that when the voice is screaming, we suddenly hear a wall of static that, upon further investigation, consists of cymbals and guitars. But they don't really sound like good cymbals and they don't really sound like good guitars. It's as if the soundstage, if you can even say there is one, collapsed and got filled in with static. The snare drum is always even. And the voice is always even. And the bass is even. Everything is always even. It simply fills in the box in which it exists. It is all very skillfully articulated, even with the cymbals and the guitars sounding like static. But it's uninteresting. My reaction isn't like my grandparents' holding their hands to their ears and saying, "Turn off that Beatles crap." It's not that it's offensive to me. It's that it's boring. And you don't want to spend time in a studio controlling and thinking things to death in order to make them uninteresting. That kind of wild-man effect, of things getting smashed around in an uncontrollable way, created surprises. And it created things that were illogical. When it's illogical, that's when feelings happen. Because when logic is happening, you aren't feeling. If you let illogical things happen, you're giving nutrients to the listener for their feelings to become engaged.

Take Steely Dan, for example. Even in their kind of "perfection," there is something in the vision that still is engaging and off-kilter enough. It might be something as simple as the wildly nuanced horn charts on *Gaucho*. It might be the fact that on "Time out of Mind" or "Hey Nineteen," there are huge holes of silence. And there are chordal clusters, so distinctively themselves, which don't sound like every other band. You become engaged in that thing that is unique. If you see them live they're different each time. And with their band, as tight as they are, you can feel that every musician is pushing boundaries. It is something very tangible and far more interesting than watching a band that is acting like it's rocking and overselling. I get the same reaction when I listen to Jerry Lee Lewis at the Star Club, throwing down on "Money." His band is hanging on by the seat of its pants. He's just like a wild bull.

I appreciate when a client brings a project to me and says, "Here's a Black Sabbath album and here's a Green Day album. I want to sound like that." By then I will have heard the clients' songs and seen them live. Usually, I'm blissfully free of the influences of those albums they bring to the table. So I'm just listening to *them*. And I try to protect myself. If they say "Green Day and Black Sabbath," it gives me a sense of something sonically or emotionally that touches them or fuels them. And that might be useful information. But I really just say, "You know, this is *your* session. It's not a Green Day session. And I want what it is that *you* do, with all of your beautiful limitations. We'll try to capture the sparks of those things that are uniquely you, and priceless, and render them in a way that's going to communicate that special essence to listeners."

I don't want to spend my time with projects that are simply going to *waste* time, so I don't work in the studio nearly as much as some people. I've learned over the years to be very careful, a good listener, and try to nuance my suggestions or responses in ways that leave others with a sense of their dignity. If I don't feel like I get what the artist or band is about, what I increasingly say is, "Sorry, but I'm not the right guy for this." I do that a lot, especially if it's an artist whose whole drive seems more about the need to be appreciated and "making it"; where it's more, "Purple is going to be big next year and I'm more purple than that is, right now, so let's do it!" Unless purple feels really true to me, and it feels like it's coming from a true place in them, I'm just not interested. It might be great music for someone else and there may be millions of people who *are* touched by it. And that's why, instead of critiquing it, I'll just put it on me and say, "I'm the wrong guy for the project." It's a big world out there. There are people who will never "get" Picasso and there are people who are moved by him. There are people who find Schoenberg an exercise in twelve-tone self-absorption and other people who listen to the *Genesis Suite* and feel he put it on the line, risked something.

to those recordings and you just *feel so good*. Why? Because you can actually feel *humans*, you can feel the people, you can feel the interaction. As a listener, you feel the humanness.

But as the world progressed and technology advanced, you moved more and more away from that. And what happened is, the equipment started changing with it, along with the world. The equipment, just as music always does, reflects society and where the world is. And the farther technology got, the more lonely I think people got.

Now they're making equipment with so many bells and whistles on it that you don't hear the humanness. So even the equipment today is a reflection of where society's at. We want stimulation—now-now-now, bam-bam, pizzazz, wow-wow-wow—reaching to the stars. And instead of looking outward, instead of looking through a telescope, you should be looking back through microscopes, looking *inward*. It's all in us.

My brother is a psychoanalyst. He had three patients that came from affluent families, who were so lost, socially, that they'd simply *leave the house* and they were lost. These kids joined a gang. Rich kids joining a gang. And to do anything there, you had either to do a drug deal, commit a crime, or even as much as murder, to belong. His opinion is that these people were looking for *something* to belong to.

Kids are just trying to survive, but they don't know, and people are only starting to realize the ramifications of this: kids getting fat, eating fast food, junk. We're an obese society with an epidemic of diabetes. This society, our richest country in the world, should be advanced. The cheapest health care you can get is to spend money to eat right and take care of yourself. Pay now or pay later. Take care of yourself.

It used to be that, if you didn't have TV with hundreds and hundreds of channels and the computer as your means of stimulation, you had to go out and play with kids, play sports, play in bands. You looked for things to do to give you that human gratification, engaging with people, being in a team, a playful gang, buddies, making up games, in the woods, in the fields, back yards, fantasies, basketball, football, music—whatever it might be. I was seven nights a week in a band. Seven nights a week, that's all you did!

Not only has the technology isolated people from being together, but you feel it, it sounds like it, and I think a lot of the music you listen to today makes you feel lonely. You hear it and it's stimulating, you've got all the samples, you've got everything lined up and it seems—whoa, that's amazing!—and you're impressed because we're human, we're *not* perfect. So you're striving to be perfect. And Pro Tools makes it possible for things to sound perfect. But, in the end, you're left lonely because what you're missing is that interaction.

A kid invited me to hear his song. It was all done on Pro Tools. He did everything. He said, "What do you think?" I said, "It sounds stimulating, it's powerful, it sounds perfect—but I feel *nothing*." He said, "Really." He was nervous and he said, "What do you mean?" I said, "I don't feel any connection. I don't feel anybody connecting with anybody. I don't feel any integration. I don't feel anything." And then he said, "What should I do?" That tells the whole story right there.

He didn't even know what to do. So I said, "Why don't you start by trying to have two people play together; have one person, a guy like me, come in and try to make it sound like playing with *people—something reacting to something.* You've got it all good, it's all perfect, but I don't feel anything."

And that's why bands like Led Zeppelin sound amazing, still. Because they played the songs, they listened to one another, they reacted to one another. The big thing is that they were playing together. You could go see seven shows and all seven shows would be different. Because they knew how to play off one another. It wasn't just about them. They weren't just trying to be a machine. They were reacting to one another and playing together. It was a human thing. I think that's what's missing in music and it's only a reflection of what's missing in the world. It's all tied in.

I have a Zeppelin band and I take it super seriously. I wrote out the parts (as much as I could, understanding Bonham) and I memorized all the songs, but I have to practice the day before and the day of the gig. Even if I'm doing sessions, I'll practice at two in the morning. There's no substitution for practicing, practicing, practicing. There's no substitution for hours and hours of learning your instrument. It's about putting in the time. Every song is so complex; Bonham's feel and technique. Those songs are great compositions and you have to understand composition. You have to be able to count the right tempo off, then you've got to play with the right feel, then you have to play the parts, *then* you have to be able to *listen* to everybody to make it sound right—together.

Then you have to be able to improvise—*improvise, folks.* That means: listen, play the parts, play in time, play with feel, listen, and react.

Every song's another movie. And I'm an actor in all the movies. It's really difficult. We play an hour and forty-five, nonstop, and I am whooped. I bring my gear, there's no tech. I wait till the band before me is done playing, I walk up onstage, I set up. I don't even look at the audience, I don't talk to them. Once I get the gear taped down, I start "Good Times, Bad Times." When I'm done, I pack up. I don't care who's in the audience. I'm doing it for the experience. And it kicks my ass. It's the hardest gig I've ever done. You go from "Good Times, Bad Times" into "The Ocean" to "Rock and Roll" to "The Rover" to "Heartbreaker" to "Whole Lotta Love." The tempo to "Dancing Days": if you do that too fast, or too slow, it's all wrong, especially too fast. All these songs, if done too fast are wrong. "Immigrant Song," everybody thinks is fast. It's not. Or "The Ocean": I never play it slow enough.

I'm not ready to retire. A lot of people constantly, from day one, are looking to slow down, to retire. I'm not putting anybody down who wants to do that. But I'm not ready to sit back. I'm still trying to be aggressive.

You do this music because you love it. That's big.

And you have to do it with something technology can't give you: truth and honor.

Remember: we were designed to touch, embrace, and feel.

Less Noise, More Soul

by DAVID FLITNER

I f you want to make God laugh, it has been said, tell her your plans. The arrival of digital technology for music production was thought to herald a new era of aural possibility, with attendant sales, comparable to the leap represented by the displacement of wax cylinders by recorded discs. Yet the contemporary era is characterized by an ability to make better and better representations of less and less substance; when, arguably, there is the potential for our fascination with the *tools* of creativity to overwhelm our sense of the *essence* of creativity. When, indeed, it is increasingly possible to construct musical production so perfect it lacks the beauty, intrigue, and welcome seduction of mystery; when any number of genre-defining songs simply would not sound like themselves if they were produced today; when a ring tone can top the UK charts.

John Lennon had it right: "Life is what happens to you while you're busy making other plans." The road to the new paradigm is defined by shifts and omissions, trends and illusions. It involves natural changes in taste and stunning unawareness of consequences in the realms of composition and performance, and in production which has become "colonized by technology." The unavoidable question becomes: It's better production, but is it better music?

Because of the sine qua non role of the Beatles this essay will refer frequently to their work (and that of other groundbreaking artists of the 1960s) as it explores these issues. This is by no means to suggest theirs was, or is, the only work worthy as a reference point. Great music is unconfined by time, place, or genre and it is hoped the reader will immediately be aware of his or her own examples. But the truth is, we would not be having this discussion if it were not for the Beatles, George Martin, and their production team. As Ian MacDonald has so succinctly put it, "The Beatles' way of doing things changed the way things were done and, in so doing, changed the way we expect things to be done. That the future is partly a consequence of the existence of the Beatles is a measure of their importance."

The conversation begins with composition. Musician John Domaschko points out that popular music managed to move from the Everly Brothers' "All I Have to Do Is Dream" to Jimi Hendrix's "Purple Haze" in nine years. If this doesn't qualify as a genre revolution, one would be hard pressed to say what does. The indispensible elements were sociological ferment, imagination, and growth. The voices were those of the composer and performer. And the vehicles were facilities

from the primordial glory of Sam Phillips's Sun Records to
Berry Gordy's Motown to 3 Abbey Road. Quality composition propelled music into a new realm of social significance
despite what would now be seen as the numbing limitations
of the equipment which captured the sound. Never mind.
As Stephen St. Croix said, of this dynamic elsewhere, "The
recordings are pretty crappy. But the music, the arrangements,
the execution, the intensity, the pain, the pleasure, the whole
story—this is music, this is quality, this is history, this is art."

Listen to the subtle and extraordinary chord change in the
second bridge, just prior to the final verse, of Roy Orbison's
classic "Oh, Pretty Woman" ("'Cause I need you/I'll treat
you right..."): the move from F-sharp minor to D minor
rather than the assumed (even anticipated) conventional D
major. Or consider the unexpected tension of the G bass
note, twice suspended in midair, in each verse of the Beatles'
"In My Life" and then the descending chord and melody
structure at the conclusion of each verse, F-sharp minor–B–
D minor–A, one of the most gracefully resolved sequences
in modern music. The Byrds' "Everybody's Been Burned"
and Simon and Garfunkel's "The Dangling Conversation"
are other examples among many. Explore, as well, the rapid
artistic development of the band Love over the course of
three increasingly complex and even visionary albums in just
two years between 1966 and 1967.

Additionally, there is the often overlooked aspect of
dexterous use of language, a value celebrated by the Beatles,
Bob Dylan, Joni Mitchell, Love, the Byrds and, more recently,

Lyle Lovett and Patty Griffin. This capacity plays no small part in the construction of music that retains relevance over time.

What these amount to, even in supposedly simple pop songs, is sophistication. This reflects—indeed, requires—an open sensibility and time and effort. The Beatles' recordings gathered as *Anthology* demonstrate, unequivocally, the virtue of "growing" a song. But if the compositional process is reduced to laying down an infectious guitar line or a dance rhythm, to which players and vocalists basically riff, or if it primarily involves hitting Play on a sequencer, or reliance largely on the addition of snippets from previous recordings, the likelihood of sophistication emerging, while present, is decidedly less. This is not to imply that something very good to listen to cannot arise from these latter techniques, only that it is less likely to be interesting beyond a certain and narrowly circumscribed cultural time frame. Again, this is why so many seemingly "primitive" recordings from the '50s and '60s remain compelling. Memorable music is not dependent upon great technology but it does depend upon great creative energies.

Lasting music may also benefit from an awareness of roots. Numerous artists have made clear that one's work often represents an adaptation of what came before and even a cross-pollination of sources. Keith Richards regularly honors Robert Johnson. Roger McGuinn has acknowledged influences as diverse as Bach and Coltrane, while Los Lonely Boys pay open homage to Ritchie Valens. In no creative form can ignorance or conscious disregard of that form's heritage be considered acceptable. What credible writer is unaware of Dickens? What painter knows nothing of Van Gogh? Pop, even as it is a vehicle of youthful identity and rebellion, nonetheless risks inadequacy, if not irrelevance, without the leavening of revolution with evolution. It is simply not good enough for artists, engineers, producers, or labels to work without reference to the chronology of their own form. There is no requirement that new work must resemble that of the past but knowledge of the past can make new work richer. And, as MacDonald has argued, "If one has nothing excellent by which to compare something of lower value, one won't notice that one is being short-changed."

Inextricably linked to any definition of quality composition is melody. And here rock, particularly, has been straddling a chasm of divergent-yet-complementary energies almost from the beginning due to the diverse sources of its conception. Rock is, quite literally, inconceivable without the African American experience. What the latter brought to the germination of the form is irreplaceable and its presence in composition, presentation, and production continues intact. But what many observers fail to remember is that the full flowering of rock would not be what it is without the vital additional influences of pop, folk and country. To neglect a complete analysis is to truncate appreciation.

Hagiographic accounts of rock's blues origins are not so much inaccurate as they are insufficient. They cannot explain the extraordinary diversity of textures and stylistic flourishing of a genre which encompasses both Nirvana's "Smells Like

Teen Spirit" and the Eagles' "Desperado." (It is more than a little difficult to imagine what exactly might be the blues roots of the Beatles' "She's Leaving Home" or the Beach Boys' "God Only Knows.") And the loosening of these familial ties has contributed in no small way to a decline in melodicism.

By the 1990s, the rise of grunge and various offshoots of metal signaled the supremacy of increasingly angst-driven abstractions of blues-based rock, decreasingly reliant on melody (even the hair bands of the '80s made significant use of melody), and subject to ever more standardized production techniques, tools, and sounds—much of which was largely displaced by the energy and ethos of hip-hop. Meanwhile, a good deal of melody, and to no small extent much of the pop-rock idiom, migrated to country.

Blues-based structures are far less dependent on melodic invention and far more on veracity of expression. Seriously exciting rock has been built on the blues tradition, as everyone knows, from Led Zeppelin to AC/DC to Stevie Ray Vaughan. But except for their application in the most deft and authentic of hands, these structures can verge on minimalism and the merely simple. This may reflect a cultural comfort level with a very American form but it may as easily reflect its sheer convenience as a delivery vehicle. And especially when a tune is going to be cut and pasted and fed into the meat grinder of Pro Tools, it can be tempting to neglect wrestling with nuance and complexity.

At best, what is sought is a process, to use Howard Bilerman's phrase, of "organic growth." The right choice of chord changes and phrasings; the integrity of unadulterated human voices; an obbligato that, even if beguilingly simple, enhances the emotional experience; a lyrical message that speaks of enduring issues: these are all about good, even inspired, creative judgment and about avoiding what Chet Baker described as the danger of having "a lot of technique and no soul."

The more generations which have grown up with a proficiency in the norms of rock, the easier it has become to believe that good music is largely about playing off a groove with slick chops and cutting-edge gear. A hot tune, then, may be defined by displays of performance prowess on both sides of the studio glass. But, as MacDonald asks, "Does it *mean* anything?" Because the truth is that "the intensity of experience which is the foundation of serious music" has far less to do, inherently, with style points and everything to do with essential human feeling: Does it touch listeners? Does it make them want to scream or cry, or fill them with a greater sense of the gift of love? Does it reflect something truthful? Will it be worth hearing in twenty years?

Underlying much of this is the application of sheer hard work. The work of the artist is at least as grueling, essentially demanding and daunting, as that of the individual in the conventional sector, a point which is easy to miss, if not dismiss. Because the artist is in full-time session with the human psyche, he or she is *always* working. And attempting to engage, in the best moments, honestly with what is human.

Who *wants* to do this? How many people *like* looking in the mirror for prolonged periods? We're not talking here about narcissism; rather, a journey of discovery. It is thoroughly unrelated to time clocks. It is continually under way. And it can be as painful as it is occasionally exhilarating.

Is this always done with integrity? Is everyone engaged in this work conscious of its depths and the responsibility that is necessary? Unlikely. It is quite possible that a young artist, resplendent in tattoos and body piercing, may have only a faint sense of the inner reaches with which he or she is dealing. And, clearly, anyone can use art as an excuse for indulgence at the sensory level. Art, truly met, obliges an unflinching commitment to examine and touch that which other areas of life and livelihood must subjugate. One may come up short, again and again, but the job requires unrelenting intent.

One of Rilke's great friends and benefactresses wrote to him, "If you were not so desperate you probably would not write so wonderfully, so be desperate! Be really desperate!" And Daniel Barenboim argues that "one needs to have a great life experience to be a good musician." The courage to run this gauntlet is, time and again, demonstrated in memorable music. But it cannot be contrived and it is not the product of the click of a mouse. It is its very individuality, which then speaks to other individuals, which contributes to its being art.

Perhaps there is an unrecognized hesitancy which attends having grown up with Great Works already an assumed aspect of the landscape and that, even on an unstated basis, leads one to conclude, "Why bother trying to compete with Lennon and McCartney, Brian Wilson, Simon and Garfunkel, Holland-Dozier-Holland, or Jimi Hendrix?" (As writer Jim Harrison has said, recalling contemplation of beginning his first novel, "My proper sense of intimidation came from having read the best.")

It is also possible that composers are either unfamiliar with earlier works or are unmoved by them. Tastes, sensibilities, and fashion all change in response to market driven promptings and societal reality. And it is not impossible that some degree of correlation exists between familial dislocation having become a statistical likelihood for many in U.S. society, and the growth of forms of expression reflecting anxiety, rootlessness, and the nonmelodic. In part, naturally enough, there is the time-honored process of rejection of parental tastes. Therefore, if the older generation embraces melody the only appropriate stand is the embrace of the nonmelodic, just as the only alternative to (once rebellious) long hair having become mainstream was the shaved head. But, more pertinently, it may be harder to be moved by paeans to innocent love (or the merely subtly titillating) when what a developing psyche experiences, day to day, are significant doses of environmental coarsening, stress, and profound distractions of commerce and imagery. Technology cannot do much here, of course, except perhaps that the people using it might want to be circumspect about applying it in ways that make things worse.

As well, there is the irony that the general relaxation of social constraints on the individual in the West has meant, in an almost Jungian dynamic, a decrease in the kind of substantive individualism that rises to confront such constraints. And, of course, there is the almost unstoppable force of the transition from the aural experience, to the predominance of the visual, in cultural media. That these phenomena, hard to define though they may be, have had a dulling impact on the nourishment of powerful music, is highly likely. Aaron Copland put it thus: "When the audience changes, music changes."

The delivery of quality composition depends ultimately upon quality performance and production. And here arise some of the most problematic aspects of the process. Respected engineer Bruce Swedien establishes the premise when he insists, "Memorable recordings start with purely emotional values, not technical values." To which St. Croix adds a sobering dictum, "The best gear increases your chances of more quality product, but only if you already have what it takes. If you don't it only helps you produce slicker crap." But the contemporary era offers nearly irresistible options for altering music, taking it to unimagined territory, circumventing requirements of talent, and shrinking the artist to a hollowed-out delivery mechanism, just one more ingredient in the recipe. As distinguished pianist and writer Charles Rosen observes, "All forms of culture, of course, can turn into nonsense or become meaningless acts carried out almost mechanically, but few arrive at the intense inane so easily as music..."

The conversational default setting here is the Beatles' critically formative experience in Hamburg, Germany, what has appropriately been referred to as the band's "baptism by fire." There is no substitute for immersion in this crucible, the process of forging creative skills under demanding, even stressful conditions; when you learn, as Gateway Mastering's Tom Ryan has said, that you can either "fall on your face or be appreciated in time." Technology, ironically, offers the option of avoiding all this. Which means that, both figuratively and physically, nobody has to go to Hamburg anymore. And thereby is lost an essential aspect of the learning and cohesion necessary for great and serendipitous human collaboration.

The joke amongst many audio professionals in the Pro Tools world is, following one take, pleasantly to tell the artist, "That sounded sh---y. Come on in and have a listen." The inference is that you don't have to *be* good, you just have to be helped to *sound* good. And to the extent this becomes largely about facility in manipulating ones and zeroes it radically shifts the locus, if not the definition, of musical creativity to where, as John Domaschko suggests, "Today, *production* has become the art."

But performance does not necessarily have to be perfect to be right. Nor is it improved by the imposition of audio uniformity on the work of individuals. Much current commercial recording sounds alike and indistinct because of the almost eerie similarity of the sonic sheen in which song after song, from one genre to another, is wrapped; a veneer of bright, polished "perfection" done with industry-standard tools. What's missing is the sense of what's human: real people, with their own subtle idiosyncrasies of articulation or instrumental prowess, in concert with other, equally individual band members. There might even be mistakes! Or, at the least, beautifully unintended outcroppings as these human players make their simultaneously mutual yet individual journeys through a song. George Martin has written, "I am not sure how much cold-blooded analysis has to do with one's passion for a work of art. It is a bit like falling in love. Do we really care if there is the odd wrinkle here or there? The power to move people, to tears or laughter, to violence or sympathy, is the strongest attribute that any art can have." And Beatles engineer Geoff Emerick reports that the band was "constantly in search of perfection, it's true, but they were looking for the perfect way to convey a feeling, not technical perfection, which seems to be the goal of many of today's records. If someone made a tiny mistake or sang something a little funny in a Beatles session, it would generally be left in if it was felt it added to the character of the record. Sometimes we'd even accentuate the mistake during mixing, just to underline the fact that the music was being made by fallible human beings." "I never made money on a 'perfect' record," R&B artist Otis Williams said. "The records that sold always had some flaw." The perfection of *im*perfection.

Bobby Frasier has gone so far as to argue the paradoxical likelihood that even if the Beatles *had* Pro Tools it would not have meant better music. Indeed, George Martin feels *Sgt. Pepper* would not have been as good if it had been done on a twenty-four track recorder since, as Emerick says, it was the very limitations which both necessitated and inspired creativity. Their work was fundamentally an act of imagination: drawing upon an array of genres yet making the results sound very much their own; utilizing unexpected combinations of instruments; resorting to techniques thoroughly outside the box such as clipping sections of a recorded track, throwing them in the air, and splicing pieces randomly to form a new backing track; playing the solo to "Nowhere Man" on two Stratocasters thereby, for all practical purposes, anticipating chorusing. There is a vast qualitative difference between having thought to do this, in the first instance and, in later history, pushing a couple of buttons on a multieffects processor. The former is revolution, whereas the latter is formalized institution. (Indeed, if digital recording tools are such an incontrovertible indicator of success, why are so many processing devices touted for their ability to restore "analog warmth" to the signal path, a trend that reached a sort of apex with the introduction of a processor designed to simulate the sound of *tape*?)

For a recent demonstration of the fearless embrace of the potential of the unadorned, one need look no further than the stunningly low-tech and honest collaborations of Johnny Cash and producer Rick Rubin late in Cash's life—grippingly relevant bare-bones music that makes others' reliance on pitch correction, embellishment, and demographics seem embarrassing. If everything is "leveled out," we remove ourselves from the revelatory possibilities of experiencing the contrast between low and high moments. Removal of the dark does not necessarily improve our experience of the light.

The very sounds of performers can find themselves diminished through the smothering application of processing to fit de rigueur parameters; for example, the ubiquitous heavily compressed and distorted guitar, and featureless chugging bass, often largely indistinguishable in character from the kick drum. Ray Manzarek's piano bass had a distinct sonority utterly unlike Noel Redding's bass, which in turn was nothing like Jack Bruce's or Jack Casady's or Chas Chandler's, Chris Hillman's, Ken Forssi's, James Jamerson's, or Pete Farndon's. There was no one-size-fits-all regimentation of instruments. More often than not, players sounded like individuals and a band was worth listening to for its parts as well as its whole.

It is often noted that a finely composed song is capable of being performed by a single voice accompanied by a single instrument and will sound just as good as it does when immersed in production. Yet now when an artist sits down with an acoustic guitar and his or her own voice, he or she may sound more interesting than with accompaniment. In a 2004 promotional clip depicting soundtrack preparation for a remake of the '60s film *Alfie*, Dave Stewart and Mick Jagger were shown discussing a song featuring Jagger's vocal work. At one point, the two musicians simply played rudimentary guitar chords and Jagger sang. Voilà. A real and recognizable sound immediately caught one's attention, recalling, if anything, the raw flavor of an early Rolling Stones record. Suddenly the camera cut to a mixing console as all the pre-recorded tracks for the song were brought up to display what quickly became a standard rock-based movie theme with standard rock instrumentation.

Being distinct is frequently about being tasteful. Guitar pyrotechnics and vocal gyrations, for example, may as easily mask, or distract from, a lack of substance as be carriers of soaring splendor. Essence and integrity are neither decibel- nor mile per hour–specific. Percussion great Kenny Aronoff tells drum clinic audiences, "No two people play the same thing exactly alike, so excess is not required for individuality." Billy Bremner's understated guitar solos on the Pretenders' "Back on the Chain Gang" are case studies in elegant simplicity even as they are individual, as is James Honeyman-Scott's opening solo on that band's "Kid." George Harrison is remembered as a great guitarist not for awesome technical prowess but because of the beauty with which his work supported the Beatles' songs. Not every player is a Jaco Pastorius or Edward Van Halen and not everyone needs to be. They must, however, be themselves. The fact is, individuality is revealed in simplicity—as "simple" as a piece by Satie. The big, almost adolescent lie, as it were, is the imagining of complexity as implying greater difficulty or better music per se. Because the real difficulty resides in the expression of honest feeling. As Bruce Swedien says, "To me, to be important, a popular song must make a spiritual connection with the listener. Its true value lies not in the vocal acrobatics of the performer, but in what the performer's musical statement declares to the soul of the listener."

This is not an argument for sloppiness or to suggest that primitiveness is somehow to be preferred over refinement or dexterity. Indeed, an unschooled musician, engineer, or producer runs the risk of ignorance of options and a resultant ossification of thinking and presentation. But overreliance on chops, plug-ins, and digital manipulation is equally capable of leading one astray, when the correct answer to a complex creative question may be the simple one.

What is desired here has been succinctly stated by music retail executive Christopher Gleason: "a sound that is pleasing." This is so deceptively simple even as it is so unquantifiably elusive (one knows it when one hears it!): a fortuitous congruence of creative ideas, human musculature, hand-eye coordination, strings, guitar architecture, vacuum tubes, amplifier circuits, mic placement, mixing medium, studio design, mastering, disc manufacturing, speakers, ears, and heart; a highly personal transaction, when it is successful, between artist and listener.

Swedien reflects, "The old musical instrument makers didn't measure—they just listened," adding that Stradivari "didn't have a computer. Perhaps his violins would not have been as wonderful sounding if he had had a computer."

Timbre and feel may matter as much as message. Indeed, they may *be* the message. All sorts of memorable pop hits are characterized by infectious tones and hooks, both vocal and instrumental. And sometimes a listener just wants some fun. Diversion is one of music's historic and legitimate functions and only a snob, whose consideration of music resides in the abstract and the effete, who has never cut loose on a dance floor, or has never been privileged enough to get lost in the collaborative joy of making music on stage for a pumped up crowd at midnight on a Friday could fail to know this.

Listen to the clanging cowbell—undeniable—leading into and out of Mountain's raucous, blues-based "Mississippi Queen." Or to any number of mid-'60s releases from Stax/Volt that seemed almost to celebrate mic bleed and over-driven inputs. Or to the insistent combination of drums and dual basses which pulse right from the top of Don Henley's (nonetheless lyrically significant) "All She Wants to Do Is Dance." Or to the irrepressible exuberance of Manfred Mann's "Do Wah Diddy Diddy." And then, for good measure, put on the Standells' prepunk "Sometimes Good Guys Don't Wear White." The snare pounds away, sounding almost as if the drummer were battering a particularly sonorous upended garbage can. The effect is powerful and largely serendipitous, which is precisely the point.

In 2005, Land Rover used "I'll Travel," by a nearly unknown '60s band, the Sonics, as the backdrop for one of its commercials. The startlingly energetic and ragged song is, by today's standards, dreadfully recorded. Perhaps this was seen as a good marketing choice because simply hearing it is experientially more interesting.★

———

★For years, rock artists resisted the very idea of licensing use of their work in commercials, an application which was seen as a near moral violation of creative integrity, inasmuch as a piece of music was felt to have an inherent importance that would be qualitatively reduced in such a context. Today, while there remain holdouts, such a decision is viewed as involving nothing more than simple commerce. While it is demonstrably true that the ardor of all revolutions tends to fade—and that modalities and necessities for reaching an audience inexorably change—this nonetheless reflects a definitional alteration whereby popular music is no longer conceived as intrinsically significant; rather, as a soundtrack for fashion, promotion, and lifestyle. This matters.

Why is the unembellished now thought to be insufficiently interesting? Would pitch correction have improved Bob Dylan? If the rough and elemental classic "Gloria" by Van Morrison and Them had been recorded today, any distortion would be intentional and, yes, refined; there would in all likelihood be far more tracks; and a polished gloss would overlay the finished product. And a song which helps define rock and roll might go unremarked. The near compulsion to process, tweak, and homogenize in the interest of the marketably safe and familiar reaches the point of engendering the merely mundane, an irony acknowledged by engineer Chuck Ainley in a comment about recording the clearly recognizable guitar of Mark Knopfler: "In fact, the more processing you do, the less unique he becomes."

John Phillips, whose vocal arrangements for the Mamas and the Papas rivaled those of Brian Wilson for the Beach Boys, spoke of "the Fifth Voice: the ringing, resonant overtones that vibrate through the harmonies and into your limbs and chest when they are perfectly tuned." Every musician worthy of the name has known this sensation. But note the use of the word *perfectly*, because this is a description of a qualitative experience incapable of being rendered by "perfectly" calibrated software: it must be *felt*.

The need, ultimately, is for balance between the ineffably human and the imaginatively mechanical. Thomas Merton averred, "Technology was made for man, not man for technology." Thus, the search must be for a positively integrative audio, for durable goods which grow out of an enlarged paradigm, and which recognizes the appropriate tension of opposites. Seamless demonstrations may be heard on Chris Isaak's "Wicked Game," a song that comes across completely naturally yet which is replete with judicious technical adjustments, and in Eric Clapton's lustrous and enhanced album *Pilgrim*. It is no longer a question of either/or, but of an artistic both/and. As Chet Baker said, "If it *sounds* right it *is* right." No one is going back to wax cylinders or tube-based consoles, but everyone involved must examine the implications of Ian MacDonald's critical observation, "The difference between Sixties pop and what came after it are epitomised by the loss of one vital element: the unexpected." The endless search for perfection *is not necessary* to the extent that it reduces such possibilities.

In May 2003, after nearly forty years, the Beatles' music carried Paul McCartney to a performance before 100,000 people—many of whom sang along in English—in Moscow's Red Square. McCartney was welcomed by Russian president Vladimir Putin, and when he asked whether the latter had listened to the Beatles while growing up within the strictures of the Soviet system, the former KGB officer said, "Your music was like an open window to the world."

Such music, at special moments, reflects the language of our essence. Ringo Starr recalls, poignantly, "I do get emotional when I think back about those times. . . . We were honest with each other and we were honest about the music. The music was positive. It was positive in love. They did write—we all wrote—about other things, but the basic Beatles message was Love." One should not underestimate the artistic and social power of such a creative message, particularly since it was accomplished in an era so heavily characterized by challenge and change.

At the same time as the Beatles were exploding across the American cultural landscape, Senator J. William Fulbright said this: "We must dare to think about 'unthinkable things,' because when things become 'unthinkable,' thinking stops and action becomes mindless. . . . we must think and talk about our problems with perfect freedom . . ." And so it must be in the new era. The minds, the voices, the tools: they're all available. And there are millions of souls out there, loving, dancing, struggling with life and pain and hope, all waiting to hear something redolent of what is good and enduring about the human spirit.

In the onrush of a time that celebrates speed and upgrades; when the very availability of almost any new item of technology is an indication that it borders on the obsolete; when the power of immediacy makes such concepts as chronology, gradual evolution, and reflection seem almost chimerical; we may wish to consider the thoughts of writer Rick Bass: "As a tender disciple to mystery, I prefer sometimes going back after that which we've forgotten, as opposed to charging off full-tilt after something new. . . . Let's take care of and protect our wild past and remember everything within it, better to strengthen us for our race into brave new worlds."

Our ears, our brain—our heart—can tell we're hearing something that is lacking a sufficiency of the human element. We take in what we're hearing, no differently than we savor a hunk of decadent chocolate, and enjoy the moment but we don't, at some fundamental level, ever mistake it for genuine nourishment. We know we require the real thing even if, after being away from it a very long time, we almost imagine we've forgotten.

It's not the technology that's the problem; it's the ease with which it allows us to slip, step by step, away from the real, the essentially human, the necessary. Distraction has its place, but it's not art.

In the 1990s, a roughly duplicated tape surfaced. Its audio quality was decidedly limited but it contained the recording of a live solo performance by Gene Clark late in his life. Clark was the Byrds' most prolific songwriter, and as a founding member of the first significant American band to emerge in the wake of the British Invasion, had known his share of high-profile glory. Yet, years later, having repeatedly moved back in the direction of his folk and even bluegrass roots, here was Clark, plucking away at an acoustic guitar in front of what can only have been a handful of people, offering an incomplete version of a song he was still crafting—a little-known and exquisitely haunting gem, it turned out, called "Gypsy Rider"—and singing with what the word *authenticity* was coined to convey. He was doing his work, unadorned.

In the end, it was all about the music. It always will be.

The Loudness Wars: Musical Dynamics Versus Volume

by BOB LUDWIG

I've been mastering recordings professionally since the late 1960s. I would say that many of the new recordings coming to market sound worse than those made even forty years ago. They got so many things right back then, how did we go wrong? Clearly the piracy- and singles-oriented record industry no longer has the budgets to make records the old-fashioned way. Formerly, a new band often had a recording budget of $150,000 for its first album. Today, the average budget is probably less than half that. The old million-dollar-budget recordings are now a thing of the past. Artists and labels can no longer afford to hire big recording studios, staffed by seasoned professionals with well-maintained gear, for all stages of the record-making process. To save money, artists are now often recording whatever they can at their producer's home studio, or many are at the mercy of a friend who owns a Pro Tools rig in his basement yet who is not a career professional and knows little about the real craft of recording.

In addition to sounding poor, once the record is mixed and mastered, the final result is often made as loud as possible in an effort to give it a false sense of energy, an attempt to make it sound as impressive as possible.

It has gotten so out of hand that some major-name mixers who used to do unique-sounding mixes that I could pick out from a crowd of other engineers, now premaster their work merely to make it loud and compressed, just to have the mixes *approved* by short-sighted A&R executives or insecure artists. These talented mixers have seemingly single-handedly destroyed their own artistic vision to please their clients. Artists, feeling the pressure to "keep up with the Joneses," approve release versions of their music that have lost their vitality and dynamics in favor of sheer level.

The loudness wars have been going on for a long time. Here is a quote: "Volume on Records: Continental [European] recording is wanted louder than English, but care must be taken that records are not made so loud as to render them unsatis-factory from the point of wear, or make them blast on cheaper machines... It must be remembered that we are not making records for Columbia machines only." This is from the April 1930 *Columbia Graphophone Company: Recording Expeditions Instructions* manual. Before that, some needle manufacturers claimed that theirs was the loudest in the old Victrolas.

Is this extreme level ever necessary? No—all playback equipment has volume controls. Actually the engineers who manufacture radio station modulation level controllers complain how hard today's records are to broadcast without adding further distortion. The chief engineer of XM Satellite Radio told me that its broadcast codec and streaming software works much better with dynamic music. So it is all insane.

What Is *Good* About Compression?

There is almost no such thing as a great pop, country, hip-hop, or rock-and-roll record done without compression. Rock and pop music is a loud medium. Actual live performances are nearly always amplified through large stacks of loudspeakers almost always played dangerously loud enough for you to demand earplugs every time you hear live music in a stadium. OSHA★ warns of possible hearing damage with exposure to sounds louder than 85 dB sound pressure level. Rock concerts are always over 100 dB, often way over.

To make that loud sonic paradigm play on a home system, radio, or TV, the music must be compressed to some degree

---

★OSHA, the Occupational Safety and Health Administration, says that it is unsafe to be exposed for more than one and a half hours of music at a level of 102 dB, more than one hour at 105 dB, one-quarter hour or less at 115 dB, and never more than that.

to create the *illusion* of loud, big, and huge. A good mastering engineer with lots of experience can determine where the line should be drawn between musicality and impressive loudness. This is not a casual decision. As I was saying, some producers, A&R people, and even mix engineers, have taken to premastering their own mixes and blindly cranking on such devices as the Waves L1, L2 or L3 digital domain look-ahead limiters and creating special "listening mixes" that are *already* louder than a good mastering engineer might decide was good. This suicidal tendency is often going to the extreme, where in our mastering stage we will ask for preprocessed mixes to give us a chance to at least match what the engineer has sent to the A&R people, yet not have it needlessly audibly pump.

When your song is one of five hundred on an iPod shuffle, compression will make your song as loud as or louder than other songs being played, giving it more attention. The same thing occurs when comparing songs people consider buying at the iTunes store.

Well-used dynamic compression can add a lot of excitement to recordings and makes pop records more "in your face," more present. It can make a mediocre song sound much more exciting than it really is. Compression can "glue together" a rough mix. Good compression can help bring out details in a mix that would otherwise not be as audible on smaller systems. Good compression can even out mixes to make playback of a whole album more coherent and make the mixes "travel" better. With a well-compressed mix, the songs will almost sound as clear in a car doing 65 on the freeway as they do over a set of audiophile headphones (well, not really, but you get the idea).

The level wars started back in Edison's time, when certain types of playback needles would play louder than another kind. When the 45 rpm single became popular and Top 40 AM radio ruled the day, it was felt that the loudest possible single would sound better over the air. Perhaps more important when the program director was going through the stack of singles that came in that week, the louder singles, *in comparison to other records*, would make a lesser song jump out more, perhaps catching the program director's ear, and possibly leading to airplay when it might otherwise have been passed over. Those were the days the PD would add only two, possibly three new songs a week to the station's tight playlist.

The Red Book standard compact disc has a 16-bit dynamic range, or about 96 dB. This is plenty of range. As with all digital media, once the maximum level is suddenly reached, there is an abrupt stop in the system's ability to do more. Any level that tries to *go* past the maximum point is simply clipped into distortion. Instead of leaving some headroom, CDs are often mastered with the peak level being reached on every beat.

When cutting a lacquer acetate for a vinyl record release, the maximum level is not so clear cut. The maximum level depends on how long or short the program material is for a given side. How much high frequency information is being cut can limit the maximum level. If it is so intense the disc cannot be played back with a mediocre consumer cartridge, the level must be lowered, or filters to control the high frequencies must be employed. The rotational speed, 33⅓, 45, or 78 rpm, affects the maximum level as well. The maximum level is also affected by the quality of the preview system. Compared to the standard lathe that cut into a lacquer acetate, the DMM (Direct Metal Mastering) copper-cutting lathe could either cut about 15 percent more time onto a side or cut a 15 percent hotter level. The latest computer preview systems on a lathe nestle the grooves together as efficiently as physically possible, yielding either longer playing times or hotter levels. So the maximum level is dependent on many parameters in vinyl disc cutting. Unfortunately these days, due to many reasons, it isn't cost effective to cut a vinyl release from an original analog tape if one exists. Instead, almost every vinyl release I know of for the past few years has been cut from either the Red Book CD master or from a high-resolution mastering of a project, closely mirroring the CD release, be it dynamic or squished.

What Is Bad About Compression?

It is a real catch-22. When I'm doing a test mastering for a new recording, if time permits I try to give the artist and A&R people a few versions, one with dynamics as I think it should be musically, and another one louder or hotter. Most times, they choose the louder mix. When doing an A to B comparison of the more dynamic with the hotter, listening to eight or sixteen bars of each, the hotter one seems to jump out and grab your ear and the more dynamic one can sound a little wimpy by comparison. Okay, what if you made another version still 1 dB hotter? Compared to the previous hot version, the new one, on a short listen, will jump out even *more* and make the previous hot one sound inadequate. You can keep going up and up in level and, for a while, still have this "good" result. The real problem is that most A&R people, and even artists, won't compare two references by listening to them from start to finish and considering how they feel after the listen. Are their ears fatigued? Do they *feel* like listening to the album again? This is where the real musicality of an album often gets sacrificed for loud momentary excitement. Drum fills get lost, layers of guitars get pressed into a singular, ultimately boring presentation.

I often say how grateful I am that the Rolling Stones and the Beatles did *not* have these digital "look-ahead" limiters when they made their famous recordings. If their songs had been squashed to death like so many contemporary records are, they would never have had the longevity they continue to enjoy. Too much compression just sucks the life out of music; it never relaxes; it is always an assault.

When I was very young, I mastered the original vinyl cuts of *Led Zeppelin II* and *Houses of the Holy*. I never dreamed that thirty-nine years later they would still have so much airplay and still sell so many recordings. One reason Led Zeppelin has such longevity is that the band often plays very quietly, which makes the loud parts relatively much more powerful.

The whole loudness war issue is very complicated. The individual radio stations in any given market are *themselves* in a levels war with one another. Tune to a classical FM station, then tune to a pop station. While each station broadcasts with the same amount of maximum power, the pop station will always sound louder, usually much louder. If one looks at a modulation meter, a classical radio station will hit 100 percent modulation a few times per minute, if that. The pop station will hit 100 percent a few times per second! Each station's program director hopes his or her station will stand out on the dial as the listeners tune from one station to another. In the heyday of New York City's WABC-AM in the 1960s, the station used to add reverb and speed-up all its records to have its special sound.

Marshall McLuhan, in his famous book *Understanding Media: The Extensions of Man* (New American Library, 1964), coined the phrase, "The medium is the message." Pop music, broadcast over a radio or TV, is highly compressed, no matter what the content. Several generations of music listeners have now grown up listening to recordings reproduced on broadcast media rather than live. Their ears are very used to hearing heavily compressed music to the point that some listeners actually prefer hearing their favorite songs squashed on the radio instead of with the wide dynamics a good play-back system can reveal. A good mastering engineer has the objectivity that the artist and producer have often lost as to how loud, how compressed, the music should be to have the maximum excitement with the minimum negative effects.

Recently a famous heavy-metal group released a new recording that was mixed with so much compression that its fans objected and created a petition, which thousands of them signed, to have the record remixed with more dynamics. Since then, many of my clients have backed down from their previous insistence that everything be as loud as everything else and I have been able to go with more dynamic masterings. This is, hopefully, the beginning of a new era of pop music.

Forty Years of Revolution, Evolution, and Devolution: The Music Industry Ice Age—Transforming from Dinosaurs to Birds

by COOKIE MARENCO

When the agricultural revolution happened thousands of years ago, it brought commerce and trade, culture, and community. In the last two hundred years, the industrial revolution gave society machines that allowed mass production, communication, and transportation to be bigger, better, faster. Inside of a generation, the digital revolution introduced change to our now global economy so rapid and enormous that the resulting explosion of growth led to the near collapse of the world's financial system. Information can now be created, hacked, stolen, or lost at lightening speeds that seem to change our concepts of economy daily. We are bombarded with free information, not always welcomed or truthful, of which trying to manage it all seems as hopeful as lassoing a tornado.

How we deal with the mediocrity of so much information, how we organize and store it for future generations, and how we monetize the distribution of it has yet to be seen. We are witnessing the fall of the huge, lumbering corporations as they downsize to adapt to these changes and flit from fad to fad in our lifestyle.

At the time of this writing, there is a global economic crisis the likes of which we haven't seen for eighty years and which may not exist by the time you're reading this. The music recording industry is undergoing a huge paradigm shift, closely followed by the entire banking industry, both collapsing seemingly overnight. In reality, it's been a house of cards for thirty years, built by the greed of a few from the sweat of creatives and the working class. The age of digital leveled the playing field built by the corporate dinosaurs and allowed consumers to revolt with their credit cards. The fast-buck economy chose quantity over quality, credit over real cash, and a "buy-break-toss" mentality. Capitalism at its worst.

With limited spending, the future is in the hands of consumers and they speak with their pocketbooks. Who's going to enforce the laws that protect the music from piracy, when our own industry has devalued it with lackluster performances and an ever-decreasing quality of recorded sound? Can you

blame the consumer? The music industry is lucky the consumer hasn't figured out it's really paying for the radio that it
used to get for free, with a lot less hassle.

I'm not really sad about the change. Snapshots of life,
whether music, photos, videos, or news, are owned by the
people now. Old economies are gone, new ones built to sift
through the enormity of information. What used to be "who
owns it" is now "who can market it." You've got to stand by
your music and your products or fall into obscurity.

Many of us were soldiers in the army for change, preferring
thousands of indie birds instead of one big beast of a music
industry. Now that collapse is here, rebuilding an empire has
its challenges. Technology may have changed us forever, good
or bad, rich or poor, but our passion for creativity, natural
competitiveness, and striving for excellence or admiration
can't be squashed by something as mutable as technological
advances.

Twenty years ago, my title at Windham Hill Records was
A&R producer. I interacted with the artists during the development and recording of the new music they would deliver
to us, for manufacturing and distribution. Our department
was an exclusive group of six people operating out of offices
in Marin County, separated from the rest of the company
by fifty miles—and by months from when a project actually
got released. I learned quickly that you needed to keep the
marketing and sales department far, far away from any new

music in progress, or ultimately the release would suffer from the lack of an enthusiastic push to the public.

Often, part of my job was keeping the artists away from the marketing and sales department for that same reason. The artists, being understandably excited about the new music they've just recorded, want to get positive feedback for their work. If A&R was not available for instant response, the artists weren't too discriminatory about where accolades came from and the music would find its way into other departments of the company. The marketing department, naturally, was a first stop and the staff was flattered to hear the new music, feeling somewhat "special" to get it early. (People in marketing and sales always want to be in A&R.)

Promotion and publicity folks are excitable people in general—and need to be. Their enthusiasm is what can make or break an artist. Their words sell the artist's music. The artists want the world to know, and the promoters want to be the ones to *tell* the world. Back then, if the music was good, a thousand cassettes were made and distributed God knows where.

At first look, this affinity for the music might seem good. Well, it's not that simple. When the recording was completed, it still needed to be mastered, manufactured, and put carefully into the release schedule where it would have the best opportunity for maximum sales. From the time a recording was finished being mixed, there was typically a minimum of five months before the release would hit the street. First, you'd have graphics, mastering, and manufacturing to do.

Touring, end-of-year holidays, competition, or a company buyout could affect the release and postpone, by many months or even a year, a record's hitting the public.

A savvy artist manager would be able to hold the reins on the artist. But many times, without any guidance, a young artist's enthusiasm would escape the hallowed halls of the A&R office and make its way onto the listening systems of our radio promotion guy. If the music was good, the promo guy would feel privileged and somewhat naughty. Slowly, the music spread to others in the marketing department and possibly outside of the company, into the ears of DJs. Typically, radio DJs didn't care whether the recording was for sale or not and the chances of the recording's ending up on the air were pretty good. A radio DJ's job is to break new music. That's how DJs make their reputation. The downside of a leak to radio before the album is available for sale is that the artist has just wiped out his or her best chance of generating sales—when the enthusiasm is highest from the airplay.

Not every leak ended up on the air. Some fires were put out at the marketing department. If that happened, we'd issue a "cease and desist" order to stop playing or making copies. Still, when we had to revive the enthusiasm five months later, when the time for enthusiasm was ripe, the marketing department wanted to hear something new. That music they'd heard before was now a has-been. Added to this was the fact that, by now, the artist was far away from the process and onto the rest of his or her career.

Technology has changed all of that. Today, indie artists can release a recorded performance to the Internet minutes after it's complete, announce it to their fans, and have it available for sale through downloads at their own website.

Part of my job at Windham Hill was to oversee the recording process, from ensuring the music was being written, all the way through to the recording itself. Windham Hill was a label known for its quality and acoustic recordings. In the late '80s, recording devices were available that began to challenge the large, expensive studio concept. Artists saw opportunities to keep more of their recording advances in their pocket, if they could record the music in their house or home studios. Also, the mid-'80s saw the introduction of digital tape recorders such as the F-1, a device from Sony that allowed digital recording by converting video mechanisms on Betamax machines to digital audio at 44.1/16-bit CD waveforms.

The media hype for digital was beginning. We were told we could make limitless copies without destruction of the signal, analog tape hiss was eliminated, and the digital signal would last forever. It took years to find out this wasn't true and not soon enough for the public to avoid being fed these same mistruths. The public wasn't equipped to do comparative tests and accepted what the media moguls were telling them. This revolution was being led by companies wanting to sell more products to the consumers, not companies trying to improve the quality of our experience.

There were also the expensive 24- and 32-track digital tape machines from Sony and Mitsubishi, but most were out of the range of the home studio operator, costing hundreds of thousands of dollars. ADATs were soon to enter the picture, mimicking the concept of the F-1 and making 24-track digital recording available under five thousand dollars. Simultaneously, there were other formats using analog tape for multitrack recording, utilizing a variety of tape sizes ($\frac{1}{4}$-, $\frac{1}{2}$-, 1-, and 2-inch). These format wars were a nightmare. Not all studios could afford all formats, so it became difficult and expensive to transfer a project to a new studio. Some of these formats lasted only a few years, leaving the masters of this music not much more than a sand castle wiped out by a wave.

At first, my job was to ensure that the quality of a recording would be good enough for Windham Hill to release. I vetoed the first project that proposed delivery from a home recording made on a Fostex 16-track recorder, using $\frac{1}{2}$-inch tape and a noise-reduction system whose make I now forget. (This is one of those sand castle machines, by the way.) It was 1988. I thought the recording sounded terrible. The manager threatened me with blackmail on another project if I didn't accept the recording methods. I stood up to the blackmail threat, but I couldn't stop the company from agreeing to move ahead, and the project was recorded in a small flat near Venice Beach. Ultimately, the money won. Making a cheap record kept more money in the pocket of the artist (which I can't argue with) and began the delivery of substandard recordings that were still sold to the public as "high quality."

The advent of this new cheap recording solution unleashed a simultaneous flood of releases from unsigned artists working at home. And the flood of new cheap recordings caused competition for shelf space at the record stores. Year after year, more titles were released as more small labels entered the distribution system. The result was fewer units sold per title. In 1987, Windham Hill typically shipped 25,000 units upon the release of any recording. By 1990, this number dropped to less than 10,000. Today, that same recording would be lucky to ship 500 during the entire year. Sales reports from the year 2008 indicate that 108,000 unique, new titles were created—and that fewer than 6,000 of those sold more than 1,000 units.

As recordings shipped less and sold less, recording budgets began to decrease. Record labels encouraged artists to record at home to keep costs down. Understand that small labels were being paid advances by their larger distributor on each title delivered, not per unit sold. The nature of this exchange encouraged more titles, not necessarily more discrimination of quality products to the market. Unfortunately, all this choice for mediocre recordings left the public with a lackluster desire to own these new titles and sales started to slide. The public continued repurchasing their old catalog of music, and during the '90s, this disguised the truth of the matter: new music was not selling.

As a commercial label, your deal might be that the distributor paid you X-dollars for delivery of any title, in advance. In other words, you completed the recording, got it packaged and manufactured, and the distributor will have preordered it based on previous history of sales. You, the label, were paid, with a caveat that 25 percent of the money was not paid to you, to allow for returns from the store. If the title didn't sell through the initial order, the money was deducted from future payments. We called this policy the revolving-door concept. Record stores were consignment houses and not really responsible if the title didn't sell. When a title didn't, in fact, sell, the stores sent it back after a few months. Or better, they traded it for a new title, so that there was no real money exchange with the distributor. One can imagine that this was and still is a huge accounting nightmare. In some cases, it has taken years to figure out how much is owed to whom.

This often caused labels to continue offering new products, not really so much for selling, but to avoid paying back the money. Meanwhile, the public became less satisfied with the music being delivered and bought less music overall. The public made its voice heard and it wasn't going to buy the new crap the labels were putting out. Gradually, over the years, labels shipped less, more of the money was held in reserves to cover potential losses, and money was paid back to labels in lesser amounts and at longer intervals. Advances to artists, for recording at the studio, fell further and encouraged even more home recording.

Now, not every artist was capable of learning how to record. Those who were more adept began to produce and record other artists in their home at very cheap rates to supplement their incomes. By the mid-'90s, artist deals often required delivery of a completed master. Many small labels offered no advances or little money for the recording, but the artist received the label's muscle for marketing and promotion. Well, you'd hope that would happen but, truthfully, the small labels had little money for marketing and the large labels didn't care unless a record had already sold 100,000 units. Anything under that quantity was not worth pumping money into, in the eyes of the majors. The majority of the releases were little more than doorstops to keep open the bigger revolving doors of exchange.

There were exceptions to this cycle. Artists with sales of millions could often command large budgets for recording, and the "glamorous" dream of recording at established studios still swelled in their mind. Occasionally, as producers and engineers, we were offered budgets that allowed us to experience the dream as well. It was an honor to record at such hallowed places as Capitol Recording or Skywalker or the Hit Factory, or to travel to exotic locations to record a band. My own days as a rock-and-roll producer and recording engineer took me all over the world. I was grateful to have the opportunity. There is no better vacation than going somewhere to record, staying in an incredible hotel, enjoying meals at fantastic restaurants, and working with some of the finest musicians in the world—all paid for by the budget. No one goes into the studio expecting to make a doorstop. We all believe we are making incredible recordings—and many times we are. However, without some marketing, you have a doorstop—regardless of the quality—unless you figure out a way to promote it yourself, which is what many people began to do.

But big projects became less the norm and increasingly a fantasy during the '90s. The experience, the magic, and the camaraderie of making music was being replaced by musicians' working in a bedroom alone with synthesizers and computers. The illusion of self-producing a hit record persisted in the mind of many people, a lot of whom were not actually musicians, now that access to recording was easier than ever.

The downhill spiral was beginning to accelerate by the mid-'90s. Hundreds of titles were thrown against the wall, like spaghetti, to see what would stick. With the glut of easily recorded music, it became harder to find anything good to say from critics who had to wade through it all. The major labels still had millions of dollars to spend on MTV and for marketing their entertainers, while the small indie labels relied on their fans and word of mouth.

On a parallel path was the jam-band genre, bands living on playing together at events, drawing fans out of their houses, traveling to 150 gigs a year in a van with a trailer, and making a modest income. Not a glamorous life, but slightly enough above poverty to keep the dream alive. These bands sold T-shirts and other merchandise along with their CDs, and this is what qualified as tour promotion. Their events were experiences that fans could share with one another, finding relationships with others of the same mind.

Phenomena such as String Cheese Incident bubbled beneath the surface. Like them or not, heard of them or not, this was a band with thousands of fans that could fill a five-thousand-seat venue, never get a recording on the radio, receive very little press, sell relatively few recordings, but have followers who wanted to experience the live show. It was the example of what the new music economy would be and the jam-band era became both a glimmer of hope and the model we now follow for musicians wanting a successful career. Indeed, known artists whose music supplied niche audiences with some of the most incredible musicianship, creativity, and legacy began their own labels, as well, selling music, T-shirts, and memorabilia to fans. They followed in the footsteps of the jam-band artist. An independent revolution developed as the means and costs of producing products became both accessible and affordable. The Internet was growing, cell phones were on the road: we were in a do-it-yourself mode.

In the '80s, artists were prohibited from selling their recordings at shows, on the assumption that retailers would suffer a corresponding loss of sales. It was expected that labels would coordinate and pay for promotional activities that brought the public to shows and record stores. Artists made money on the tour, labels on the record sales. By the '90s, as budgets shrank for recording and cuts were made in promotion, artists argued for, and got, the ability to sell recordings at their shows. Soon a significant number of musicians made a career out of selling music and merchandise at gigs. If the label didn't supply marketing, it was a no-brainer to DIY. In fact, rather than bearing a stigma, DIY was now accepted as fate.

An additional aspect of my job at Windham Hill was to oversee the mastering process and ensure the final master was as perfect as could be. We had the great fortune of doing most of our mastering with Bernie Grundman, an incredible man with amazing ears. In the late '80s we were mastering for vinyl and cassette tape formats. The digital age changed this quickly enough. By 1988, we began releasing some titles on compact disc, and by 1990, all titles were released on CD. Vinyl died a quick death at mass distribution, not because the format was inferior, but because the CD was smaller and took up less shelf space.

The CD format gave a last breath of greed to an industry that was on its dying breath in the '80s. The business of music had become a corporate monstrosity with the ability to make a few companies/people very rich, while surviving on the talents and dreams of artists, engineers, and others at the bottom of the financial ladder. The chance that a dream would bring gold was on everyone's mind.

The reality was that music was big business and about selling units, not about art. In fact, it was never about art, and always about commerce. Any artists who think they are making art needs to get a grip and ask themselves why they want to replicate and charge money for a thousand discs. If you attach a price, it is commerce. Of course, you can be creative about commerce, and if you're smart, you learn to focus on your fans.

Big music business survived on the dream that rock and roll could be attained by the common man. Truth was, your chances were better to win the lottery. But without a few "stars," MTV, and the sex and drugs glamour of rock and roll, the dream didn't exist and the money couldn't be made.

The lure of hitting it big kept advertisers and technology companies flush, as well. Magazines that promoted music and entertainment blossomed. Technology companies, building new gear that was cheaper (but not better), accelerated the "you could do this at home" dream. CDs could now be replicated in the thousands by just about anyone with a computer and a small recording system.

Everyone dreamed of the rock-and-roll life.

In the mid-'80s, the number of small labels grew, the number of titles grew... and sales lessened per title. Record stores saw benefit in taking the same space to sell more products. From 1988 to 1990, the industry virtually changed from vinyl to CD, not so much because people didn't want vinyl, but because the stores didn't want to carry it. The CD offered more titles per space and a higher profit margin. Stores stopped ordering vinyl, labels stopped making it. The consumer never saw it coming. We were all forced to buy a CD player, like it or not, and replace our catalog of favorites with the new format.

During the '90s, the labels were revived by selling the old titles. As people replenished their collections, the labels survived and survived well. The major labels didn't have to put money into new recording, and what was left of artist development completely died. Independent labels tried to take up the slack and artists continued releasing their own recordings that they sold at gigs. The new music was being nurtured by small indie labels willing to take the chance. If an act survived, the artist might get moved up the chain and secure a major label deal. The major labels, flush with cash, became distributors, and bought and sold companies at high prices. In some ways this was a Ponzi scheme of promised futures. A few people were making a lot of money on the backs of an industry built on rock-and-roll dreams.

I remember one of the mastering sessions with Bernie, where we talked about the acceptance of "mid-fi." The public didn't seem to care that the quality of the products was diminishing, both in recording and performances. By the mid-'90s, artists and labels realized they needed a new CD to stimulate a tour. They'd deliver music with one good song on it and sell another fourteen alongside it. It didn't matter, so much, that only one song was worth listening to—it was still fifteen dollars in their pocket. What the artists and labels failed to see was that the consumer was growing increasingly tired of paying fifteen dollars for one new song. As people restocked their music collections with old favorites, new music sales were on the decline.

Well, technology waits for no man and certainly not the music business. The happy model of one song for fifteen dollars was going to be blown apart by the digital revolution, a revolution that came from the fans. The fans were the technologists who loved their music and wanted new ways to choose and new ways to find talent, or better yet, make it themselves. By the mid-'90s, it was clear that digital technology on the computer was going to be cheap enough to allow home users to make their own recordings.

Now it was true: You could make a recording at home and in your mind have access to the rock-and-roll dream. Software was developed so that you didn't even have to know how to play an instrument to record your own CD. What a thrill this was. Personalizing music! You didn't even need to buy your favorite artists' music, you just needed a few friends to play your newly found skills to. And wow! Egos rise, smiles abound, children are brilliant... it's not too late for anyone to be a star! Snapshot music.

In the mid-'90s, as the Internet revolution was taking shape, some of the fans, less inclined to be musicians, started their new music business. They began recording live shows and trading tapes for free. They'd make cassettes and CDs of their favorite music and give it to friends. Trouble was looming for the very concept of the long-playing album.

At that time, I was fortunate to work for Liquid Audio, a company that provided the first digital music downloads. The downloads could be copyright protected, put up for sale within minutes of completion, and released worldwide for distribution within a few more minutes. This was the baseball bat to the knees of the industry. While we had protection built in for the artists, companies such as Napster shot up out of nowhere and allowed free trading of music on the Internet. Despite its eventual demise, Napster leveled the playing field and the music business was changed forever.

The major labels chose to ignore the change that was coming. They were not going to alter the way they were making money and they fought the revolution of the people. Steve Jobs and Apple sided with the fans with the appearance of helping out the artists. The iPod was invented and it seemed that piracy on the Internet might be circumvented by the seventy-nine-cent download of the single.

The iPod was introduced seven years after the first digital downloads from Liquid Audio. Broadband was in most homes, Apple put millions into education and it had a great plan: The music downloads bought on iTunes, another Apple product, would only play on the iPod. It really wasn't music being sold at all: it was the iPod, an inspired move by Apple to stay afloat by appearing to sell music.

I clearly remember the brilliance of the release. One month before the iPod came to the public, Universal Music was up for sale and there was a buzz suggesting Apple was going to buy Universal Music. Something was up, but we didn't know what. Apple didn't buy Universal. It didn't buy any label. It started a revolution that led to the evolution of the music business from albums to singles. It was the 1950s music model of selling the single. Apple saw the opportunity that the major labels, in their arrogance, didn't see. Apple catered to consumers and gave them what they wanted.

By 2003 you had consumers that:

1. were growing tired of the mediocre music offered, and showed it through lack of sales,
2. didn't want to spend money on an album of songs when they only wanted to buy one single,
3. now had the Internet and new ways to find music anywhere in the world, not just at the retail outlet, and
4. had the potential to be overwhelmed by all the choices offered, get bored, and *stop buying*.

The risk of being overwhelmed by choice wasn't outweighed by the opportunity to choose new music and avoid buying what amounted to excess crap.

By 2008, the entire world economy crashed in a similar fashion to the recording industry. The banking system gave the consumers the illusion that there could be limitless spending while they dreamed of riches as fanciful as those of a rock star. And if you couldn't be a rock star, you could at least spend like one. The music industry's final collapse was already happening.

By 2008, most major labels were failing and the once grand recording studios of technology's past were being turned into condominiums. Audio engineers who had taken their studios into their home were now replaced by home operators being told that what they recorded could be every bit as good with a thousand-dollar investment. Who needs experience to place a microphone, after all? Geez, listen to the "junk" that was being turned out by the labels: a monkey could make a recording. What was the point of spending money on the music? Can anyone blame the public for revolt?

The writers who once gave us reviews and opinions, right or wrong, were put out of business, having been replaced by the fans who offered their own information on blogs and forums without being paid. Radio, magazines and music were being supplanted by the freedom of the Internet. Information was traveling at lightning speed around the world.

Needless to say, the bad recordings, sales of singles, abundance of titles, and the rapidity of the Internet clobbered change into all of us. So much information coming so fast— and at such a level of mediocrity—became overwhelming. The quality music, as of life, seemed to drop out from beneath us.

If for no other reason, labels should exist to organize music and provide ways to distinguish mediocre from great.

Now don't get me wrong. I was never happy about the record label system of old. I'm an advocate of giving away the crap for free and educating the public to my own vision of quality. Let the consumers decide. They'll pay with their pocketbooks. If used to your benefit, a label can reach any country in the world to make a sale. You can have ten fans in every country of the world and make a middle-class living, if you can figure out how to reach those fans.

It's all marketing. And, actually, it always has been. Without telling people you exist, you don't exist. Making music for your family and friends is fine, too, just like owning a camera or a basketball is part of every family's arsenal. Not everyone is going to be in the NBA.

To be an artist has always required having a personality that is resilient, able to handle criticism, and with more ambition than talent. Talent without ambition doesn't go far beyond the living room.

So…h ow do you reach the public with a truly great product?

Think pre-'60s music business. Singles, good songs with talented artists, improved sound, and quality of life. It's a smaller business of targeted niches. There is hope for the indie artist, although the money is still being made by technology companies more than by the artists. New Internet companies touting solutions to reach your fans and sell your music do little to actually promote. They offer tools and dreams that require time and money to execute, which usually must be applied by the musicians. These companies make money from investors who believe they will be the next iTunes, Facebook, or Google.

Musicians get to enjoy a life of creativity that isn't always bound by money. Hopefully, the technology companies won't be as harsh about sharing the wealth as were the record companies of old. We're in a turbulent global community that offers us access like never before. We're in a time of change and new ideas with tremendous opportunity for those who dare. The world is changing too fast to accommodate the latest trend. The creatives of today need to lead, not follow.

I have chosen to focus on what I love and appreciate most: great music, great performers, and great sound. I believe there is a niche that feels the same way I do and I look for its members every day. They might be in the USA, but could be in China, France, or New Guinea. The technology of the Internet allows me to find those people and reach them. Maybe they care about dynamics and the emotion that comes from a great recording. Maybe they want to laugh and cry, be touched in their heart and soul. At least that's what I want to hear.

Maybe the world is ready to listen.

The Problem of the Constant Upgrade

by GINO ROBAIR

C onsider the life span of the hardware we use to make and record music: pianos, guitars, saxophones, microphones, preamps, whatever. Historically, professionals and amateurs alike often used the same gear for decades. Today, however, despite the fact that music software is becoming increasingly cheaper and easier to use—even professional products—few if any of these newer tools may be said to have a similar quality of longevity.

Think about the number of computers you've owned. Do you still use the same computer, the same recording and sequencing application, and the same interface that you used ten or fifteen years ago? How about the software instruments? Probably not. Have you ever asked yourself why?

We might use the latest rev of an application that has been around for a decade, but the original versions are still on one of the many "legacy" computers parked in the garage, attic, or basement, or on the floor as a doorstop. I own several such items, few of which will actually boot up anymore. At the same time, I have a theremin from the '60s, a Fender Stratocaster from the '70s, and analog synths from the past forty years, all of which work. I know them inside and out. Yet I don't use a single software instrument, effect, or sequencer that is more than a decade old, and often they're superseded before I really get any sort of meaningful chance to explore their deeper features.

Despite the great technological strides we've made, few of us—developers or consumers—have stepped back and looked at what needs to be done to address the problems of manufactured obsolescence that we've actually come to embrace. The most fundamental of these has to do with the effect of Moore's law on music technology, which famously predicted that the number of transistors on a chip will double essentially every two years.

As processors get faster and storage devices increase in capacity (even as they shrink in size), developers continue to push the limits of technology to offer such benefits as higher resolution and more features, without raising prices. But, too often, technological advances are used simply as an excuse to launch new products with the goal of meeting the manufacturer's quarterly sales projections. For example, why was there a rush to make prosumer recording gear that supports 192 kHz sampling rates when there isn't a universal delivery system, and when few qualified mics and preamps can even pass signals that approach the Nyquist limit of that resolution?

The ultimate effect is that, in the haste to squeeze as much power out of our tools as possible, we've begun losing some of the things we took for granted when technology evolved at a slower pace, and rather than specs, *audio quality* was the primary focus. We have, in fact, sacrificed durability. Products are being made quickly and inexpensively in developing countries (a subject with innumerable additional implications) and are, to a certain extent, accepted as being somewhat disposable. As in so many other areas of the consumer market, it therefore becomes easier to replace an item, such as a keyboard controller or USB microphone, than to repair it. Consumers now accept the fact that few things are built to last, because they know from experience that the product will be superseded by something more powerful in a few months or years. Or worse, they will discover that a new operating system, or peripheral connector that doesn't support the hardware item, will become ubiquitous, making their still-working investment obsolete.

We are also sacrificing the time to become proficient with our tools. The concept of the studio-as-an-instrument, whereby a composer uses *all* the wares available to make his or her music, is a legitimate and welcome addition to the creative process. But what happens when the sheer number of important tools is updated so frequently that it becomes possible only to become familiar with a handful of them and still have time to be creative? At what point has the composer or musician had enough of acting as a technician, in thrall to the steady march of upgrades to every piece of software? When might it be acceptable simply to settle on a few *reliable* tools?

Is there a corresponding dynamic in the world of analog hardware? Certainly with any piece of hardware, you must replace parts as they wear out: vacuum tubes, capacitors, cables, strings, heads, and reeds. But in the realm of digitally constructed and processed music, the entire system is replaced with alarming regularity. It may happen incrementally, starting with a software rev, an OS upgrade, or a new computer. Or it may happen all at once, as it did when the major upgrade of my main DAW required a new computer with the latest chip *and* a new operating system. If this weren't enough, I found I also had to acquire the premium level of computer to get a FireWire port to support the hard drives that store all of my projects. But emptying my bank account was only the beginning.

Once I'd migrated my entire system to the new computer, I found that all of my audio applications needed either reauthorization or upgrading. This not only required more money, but an investment of time for loading, authorizing, and testing the software. Beyond all other considerations, this represented time away from music and work. Anyone seriously using computers for music goes through a similarly agonizing process every few years.

While upgrades are undeniably a hassle, they ostensibly permit us greater facility for getting more out of our software products, whether it's improved audio quality, additional synth voices, or deeper editing features. We accept upgrades as a fact of life, a reflection of the surging digital paradigm. Yet we rarely ask, "Why?" Or, perhaps more important, "What have we gained?"

I derive great enjoyment from the capabilities and challenges of using music technology. But what I really want to do is make music. I don't want to spend inordinate amounts of time debugging my system, nor do I want to learn a new software interface with each upgrade. Time spent hunting down an important feature hidden under a new pull-down menu is wasted creative time. I respect the hard work done by programmers over the last quarter-century; we've come a long way, very quickly. But, more than anything, I'm looking for a *musical instrument* in the most basic sense—one that I can spend the rest of my life mastering, not reconfiguring.

That same rush to get new products out to meet quarterly expectations has led many developers to deliver goods which have serious usability issues, or which lack promised features, or both. Would we put up with such a thing in a grocery store, or when we buy a car? Of course not. When it's discovered that a part in a certain model of automobile is faulty, the company announces a recall, perhaps replacing the part for free if it's easy enough to do.

Something similar occurs in the world of music software, but in this case it involves consumers actually waiting for the release of the free ".1" bug-fix to appear before jumping into any new piece of software or OS. Unfortunately, the industry is training an entire generation of users to wait for the first update before upgrading their apps. There are, of course, plenty of early adopters out there who have the stomach for blue screens and spinning beach balls. But those who have to get real work done, in real time, would much prefer waiting for demonstrated stability rather than boasting of being the first geek on the block with the latest DAW rev or software instrument.

Beyond this, and making matters worse, developers try their hardest to avoid acknowledging the issues in their products. This then necessitates trolling through user groups and online forums to see what we are up against, before investing money in a new product. And again, we have no reasonable way of knowing how long our investment will last.

Looking at it from the developer's viewpoint, there are indeed numerous system configurations, and it's impossible to address them all. Many of us know anecdotally that each person has a different user experience with a software product in terms of performance. Some of us don't get crashes, while others do. This can be blamed on system differences (e.g., which chip is in your computer), the components (interface, drives, peripherals), or the ways the application is being used. And, with limited resources, a company has to prioritize which bugs are addressed first. So, of course, when a new OS is released with little or no warning, there's a mad scramble by developers to make their app compatible, and the bug list is set under the coffee mug once again.

But wouldn't it be refreshing if developers came clean and told us what the issues are—when their products are released? Better still, wouldn't it be a win–win situation if manufacturers didn't make promises that they couldn't keep about features, only announcing things when they are fully functional, and perhaps adding extra features in .x updates? Imagine if a developer announced and delivered a bullet-proof version of its new audio app, then named five state-of-the-art features that would be added incrementally over the next few months in free updates to registered users (perhaps after they were bug-fixed using public betas).

You might ask, "What would keep the consumer from simply waiting for those five features to be added *before* buying the software, thus making the developer miss their Q1 and Q2 projections?" You may as well ask why a company would risk putting out buggy software, and incurring the wrath of its users, just in the shortsighted interest of showing a profit for a quarter or two. Because that's precisely what happens every year in this industry, often from the biggest players who have the most at stake, but which rely on their reputation as "industry standards" to carry them through problematic software revs.

In this culture of upgrades, it's time for some honest and careful reconsideration of priorities and utility:

1. I'd like the next generation of software music tools to be inspiring while staying completely out of the way of the creative process.

2. I want those tools to be intuitive, conflict free, hassle free, and most important, plug-and-play.

3. And I want to be able to pass them down to my children, just like my Strat.

Is that too much to ask?

Some Thoughts on Record Production, Its Tools, and Tomorrow's Music Producer

by SUSAN ROGERS

Record making in 2011 is essentially the same as it has been for half a century if you consider the ultimate goal and its basic concerns. The listeners' experience, however, has changed substantially; they have more options and there is greater competition for their attention and commitment. Popular music, musicians and record makers may subsequently benefit from these changes. This essay offers my view of what the art of record production aims to give to the artist and listener and what it requires from the person providing it. I will apply findings from cognitive, perceptual, and behavioral psychology to today's music listening environment and discuss what implications they have for the record producer. This generation of record makers will solve novel problems armed with traditional assets, and their recordings will contribute appreciably to popular music.

Record Production: What It Does

In practical terms, record production is the art of influencing and determining the form of a recorded musical performance to suit its intended function in the marketplace. With few exceptions, it is a collaborative activity. The producer provides an aesthetic and methodological scaffold upon which the activity is carried out. It involves both personal and practical techniques. As each actor makes a given script his or her own, so each producer makes a record that is distinct from what another would make given the same raw material. Our thoughts and emotions become the bodily gestures, facial expressions, speech, vocal prosody, and decisions that inspire and characterize works of art. The work is thus inseparable from our own experiences.

The producer's art involves shepherding several participants with a singular goal—to create a work that is viable enough to sustain itself and sprout more work in the future. Participants include the artist or band members, producer, engineer, mixer, executive producer (A&R executive or source of capital), and management. (The audience may be considered a participant to a lesser extent, but today's record-making process may include them to a greater degree than ever before, mainly as a source of capital.) Each participant contributes valuable resources to this singular goal: talent, ingenuity, ability, determination, ideas, time, and effort. So what accounts for the high rate of failure, if success may be defined as above?

Lessons from the applied mathematical field of game theory lend some insight. As implied in its name, game theory looks at how choices made by individuals affect the choices made by others in a collective endeavor. Throughout the recording process, individual motives and personal goals compete for each participant's resources; some of these can be strong enough to work against the singular main objective. Every resource, be it tangible or mental, pushing the collective to make the best possible record is countered to a greater or lesser degree by physical, psychological, and/or circumstantial factors that can foil the group's best efforts. From their initial meeting with an artist to the final delivery of the work, record producers are taking some measure of these potential impediments to better control or minimize their impact on the project.

Performance limitations can be the most conspicuous of the producer's challenges, but what constitutes a limit depends upon the height of the target. Can the artists play and sing the material they intend to sell? This is not a disingenuous question. Many attempts are required before one's best performance is delivered to a microphone; it is quantitatively and qualitatively distinct from performing to an audience. Even successful stage performers can become unnerved if they first encounter this obstacle on a recording project. Recording software allows correction of pitch and timing mistakes but the record's aesthetic will dictate whether and how much the initial gestures should be altered. The more the producer adjusts performance errors to conform to a template-based ideal, the fewer the number of expressive one-of-a-kind elements. In musical performance as in athletic performance, the failure exposes the aim. It is arguable whether aiming for a 10 and only reaching an 8 is preferable to scoring a perfectly executed 7. I agree with Geggy Tah's Tommy Jordan who said, "The wrong note played with gusto always sounds better than the right note played timidly." On behalf of the audience, the producer applies a personal aesthetic criterion for the acceptable level of shortfall. On behalf of the artist, the producer assesses the limits of each player or vocalist's capacity and evaluates performances within these limits. These criteria are covertly established early in the process and it is the producer's responsibility to consistently maintain them to reduce challenges of a second kind: the psychological.

The creative process can induce the mental obstacles of anxiety, doubt, self-sabotage, and other forms of deconstructive thinking. Some of these are well founded; we are, broadly speaking, making an unnecessary product for a vague and ephemeral buyer. To what extent do humans need art? For persons on the margins of a project whose sacrifices or resources make it possible (e.g., spouses, parents, venture capitalists), this is a thought- and sometimes criticism-provoking question. The producer assumes the proposition that the work will serve a function. One way of alleviating doubt is to show how the work functions for himself—the first listener. Confirming the validity of art with genuine praise and constructive criticism is trickier than it sounds. If it underwhelms, there are subtle but artful skills to facilitating the remedy (this topic could fill a chapter). If it overwhelms, the producer risks loss of credibility during the settling after the broom of self-congratulation has swept the room. After earning the trust of the participants, he or she can expect to occasionally have to defend it for the sake of maintaining equilibrium in the game. This is not the same as saying producers should not change their mind or admit mistakes. Self-criticism should model the ongoing critique of the work in progress. This helps establish the basic premise that there is no absolute right or wrong way to make a record; progress is made via a series of decisions based on the collective knowledge, experiences, and skills of the group. We give it our best effort using only what we have.

Drug abuse and addictions can weaken a recording project's resources by segregating the level of performance and discourse into two distinct, incompatible conditions: sober and unsober. Great recordings are exclusive to neither condition, but a recording artist with a serious substance abuse problem forces a potentially game-changing moral issue for the other participants. Harvesting inspired ideas at the cost of irreparably damaged health has consequences that extend beyond the project's completion. This cost is sometimes high enough to justify aborting a project.

The quotable Tommy Jordan said, "Music is only one aspect of my life and Geggy Tah is only one aspect of the music of my life." Creative people typically participate in more than one "game" at a time. The producer maximizes distribution of participants' resources to the game at hand. It is understood that all participants are or will be invited to make other records with other people. A potentially dispiriting impression is that these other records take priority (whether true or false) for any member of the collective. It is unsettling to watch momentum slow and morale dip when a participant's other professional goals are even casually introduced during a session. The creative balloon is a delicate thing.

It has been said that in the entertainment industry, perception is reality. Lack of money, or loss of interest or commitment from any one participant can lead to a spreading apathy for the project as a whole, undermining its perceived chance of success. Producers need to keep in mind that they are delivering their product to people (e.g., record executives, managers) who must imbue it with the same validity and enthusiasm shared by the persons who made it. Involving ancillary participants in the day-to-day progress risks their becoming overly familiar with the record to the point of apathy or at least diminishing their valuable objectivity. It is also important to remember that record makers *learn* to evaluate unfinished recordings, and that this takes skill and practice. Professional record makers assess a basic track and scratch vocal by comparing the real-time signal to a mental auditory image of what the piece will sound like after corrections, overdubs, and a final mix. It is a safe presumption that this is only achievable for those who have spent countless hours working in each of these stages. The typical A&R executive, artist management, and the project's other day-to-day "noncombatants" cannot be expected to gauge partially completed work with the same ear as can producers. Producers can use this fact to their advantage and pace when and how often they play works-in-progress outside of the studio.

Part of each producer's responsibility for overseeing each aspect of the process is to consider the context in which the recording will be heard and the various criteria with which it will be judged. There are three important audiences: the peers, the critics, and the public. Which will be most impressed? Who is the record being made for? Because each audience weighs a record's merits using different scales, rarely have artists been highly esteemed by all three audiences over the course of their careers (Duke Ellington is a rare example).

I teach at Berklee College of Music, where student producers make recordings of and for other student musicians. I am often surprised by comments these producers make about one another's work. Years of musical training, for most of them starting in childhood, have shaped their auditory pathways and their knowledge of music theory to notice subtle differences in chords and harmony that I, a nonmusician, do not notice. My for-all-intents-and-purposes normal hearing means that I can hear these differences once they are pointed out, but unless they are, they will probably escape my attention. This is anecdotal evidence supporting recent physiological findings that trained musicians have on average a higher auditory acuity than do nonmusicians. This does not mean better hearing per se; rather, a greater ability to isolate and attend to the fine details in sounds. A second important difference between a musician and a nonmusician listener is in the capacity for auditory imagery. Listening to a recording of an instrument they can play or a familiar piece of music that they have played activates the same parts of musicians' brain that are engaged when she is playing it. The fact that trained musicians have additional neural resources devoted to sound processing has implications for record producers.

The vast majority of the record-buying public are non-musicians and thus are more likely to listen synthetically to the global whole of a music recording rather than analytically to its local details. Many listeners will not respond to those musical events that may have thrilled the record's participants. Record-makers can lose sight of this fact and be tempted to gauge a record's worth by the response it gets from their peers, typically other musicians. It is indeed high praise to be called a "musician's musician" but this offers no assurance that music critics or the general public will regard the musician or his recordings as highly.

The scholarly music critic has the objective of placing the work in the broader historical context and in light of current trends. Those at the top level of critique are eminently qualified to answer the intimidating question, "Should this record have been made?" Does it represent a trend we would like to see continued? Frank Zappa wrote caustically, "We have critics to tell us whether it's any good or not, so we won't worry about that part." Right or wrong, music critics have done the work of consuming a larger than average amount of recorded music and their analyses of a record's merit in the larger scheme are informative for record makers. Even if it is accurate, a glowing endorsement does not bestow a concomitant effect on the cultural purchase of an artwork. The critic's opinion is no match for the public's, but it can ignite a movement of popular taste towards newer and more deserving works.

For optimum enjoyment, psychologists show that humans prefer a certain amount of novelty and complexity in their stimuli, balanced against a certain amount of familiarity and simplicity. Imagine a bell curve with complexity on the x axis and record sales on the y axis. The uppermost part of the curve is in the middle, representing the highest number of units sold. Let the minimum on the left represent the simplest music and the one on the right represent the most complex music. The simplest music is that which is the most predictable, best exemplified by children's music. The most complex music is the least predictable; perhaps it is free jazz. Neither form of music is ever likely to occupy the top of the sales charts.

To please a nonspecialist audience, producers critically assess their work in terms of simplicity versus complexity to gauge their product's chances at the desired height of achievement. Whether they consciously ponder them or not, two questions drive producers' aesthetic choices: Is the work original enough to entice or challenge an audience? And, Is the work familiar enough to be recognizable and memorable? Presented with a band whose work relies more heavily on technique than on the artistry of original thought, producers can introduce novelty in the arrangements, timbres, rhythms, performances, recording techniques, lyrics, or other elements. Bands whose work is avant-garde can be produced to emphasize hooks, simplify some arrangements, or clarify lyrics. (This assumes that increased record sales are the goal and that the record is not being made for a niche market that values some other quality.)

Traditionally, the availability of materials—musical instruments and players, number of tracks, square feet of recording space, and so on—imposed constraints on how the producer facilitated the recording process. Budgets determined whether the project could proceed from the vision to the materials or, if the constraints were prohibitive, needed to work from the materials to the vision. Each method has produced great recordings. Studio time aside, digital tools today allow a complicated, richly textured vision to be realized at nearly the same cost as a simpler one. Removing the old constraints has opened the floodgates to allow a higher proportion of visionary recordings than once was feasible. Yet this question persists: Is the vision of the record formed in the artist's head the one that should be made? A vision can be hard to dislodge; humans are known to be better at learning than unlearning. Facilitating the recording process requires the producer to occasionally shake the snow globe to see how many visionary ideas fall back into place. The undeniably best ideas will be preserved. (Bad ideas are underappreciated. Putting a bad idea into form can inspire by highlighting what *not* to do; the contrast can cause a good idea to emerge. At least that's a good excuse.)

How good can the record get and how do the participants know when it is done? Producers must judge the recording within the parameters they established early in the process. The artistic goal is developed in preproduction, where they learn the creative and technical strengths and weaknesses of the individuals and the collective. The question is not, "What is the best record we can make?" because it may be beyond the available resources (both internal and external) to make it. Rather, "What is the best idea, and how far can we get in realizing it?" is the gentler question that aims to push up from a baseline level of competence through eliciting the best performances and ideas from each participant. The task of producers is to find the highest musical expression inside every participant, including themselves, and draw it out. In practice, the vision is realized when the collective threshold for the proportion of original ideas and technical excellence has been crossed. Inspiration is more rare and fleeting than skill and so it is not uncommon for great recordings to feature more of the latter.

Preproduction is an opportunity for producers to critically evaluate the written material and arrangements to take stock of the record's assets. Studies of music cognition show that there are three important avenues through which a listener may be affected by music: cognitive, emotional, and motor (movement). The producer may focus on and improve the material in one or two of these areas and deemphasize the contribution from the weakest area. If the artist is exceptional in one aspect (e.g., Bob Dylan's lyrics; Brian Wilson's melodies; James Brown's grooves), the record's impact from the other two avenues may be minimal or even nonexistent.

Lyrics affect us in their power to make us think (as well as feel, which can precede, follow, or supplant thinking). It is not necessary for a record to feature great lyrics if it compensates in other areas but it must be said that it can't hurt. The producer considers lyrics in terms of the record's function in the marketplace. What might be trite to an adult could be a new idea to a teenager. When a record's lyrics do not offer the marketplace anything new or attention-grabbing, the producer builds the record on the strength of its nonlyrical elements. Mix techniques and artistry go a long way toward helping with the latter.

Powerful emotional responses to music have never depended on lyrical content. Certain melodic intervals, their progression, or harmony can automatically change the mood or physiology of listeners; they do not have to be paying attention for this to occur. (In fact, they do not even have to be human. Studies with young chickens show that behavior and neurochemistry are altered by instrumental music.) For humans, a lifetime of listening to the music of our culture builds an implicit knowledge of a music system's tonal hierarchy. Tonal schemas allow us to form expectancies for what chords will occur and when. For example, we expect certain chord progressions to eventually resolve to the tonic; if a dissonant or unexpected chord happens when we anticipated something consonant, a powerful emotion or even chills can follow. The incredible thing is that this happens even for familiar music, even when we know what to expect! Great songs are those with melodies that are emotionally affective when played without accompaniment, at various tempi, in various arrangements. If none of an album's songs pass this scrutiny, rhythm bears much of the weight of the album's emotional impact.

The power of rhythm to move us is so primal that it needs no explanation. As it relates to record sales, rhythm tracks benefit from incorporating new sounds, meters, beats, and accents to satisfy our advancing cultural expectation of novelty. Music theorists show that musical tastes evolve rapidly. Chords considered somewhat dissonant a century ago are rated as less so today. As our collective experience with music develops, the bell curve of sales as a function of complexity shifts to the right. What was once complex is eventually regarded as commonplace and thus, predictable. Producers can introduce valuable complexity to the standard pop, rock, or soul song by being rhythmically innovative. The decades-long success of hip-hop attests to how rhythmical ingenuity (coupled with socially relevant lyrics) can appeal to the public's musical appetite.

This discussion of record production has left out obligatory tasks such as organization, time management, and dispute resolution. It is more interesting to consider modern producers' responsibility to integrate their work into their artists' public profile. The traditional influences from A&R and artist management are waning in proportion to the number of recordings being made. Consequently, more producers today are overseeing or at least offering their acumen on how the recorded product relates to each artist's public image. An artist's album artwork, website design, style sense, stage presence, media awareness, and interview skills all contribute to an overall impression that can motivate listeners to identify with or dismiss that artist. Producers aware of trends in fashion, public taste, and cultural changes are better prepared to integrate choices made in the recording with the artist's public image and in so doing help foster record sales.

Record Production: What It Takes

Once the materials and infrastructure are in place, new ideas and aesthetic evaluation are what the producer primarily brings to the project. One of the biggest effects new technology has had on record production has been to shrink and mobilize the recording studio. It is still hard for many of us to accept that anyone with a computer and certain software can honestly say he or she has a recording studio. But we have to admit that this was technically true decades ago for anyone with a field recorder and a microphone, so essentially the change is not so drastic.

New ideas are the coin of the realm but the creative process involves one small part inspiration (art) and one large part technique (craft). The more technical skills a people possess, the more creative they can be and the longer they can persist when art fails them, which it will most of the time because original thoughts are cognitively more taxing than remembered skills. The record-making process does not necessarily start with inspiration. Sometimes, initiating the process will inspire a craftsman to create a work of art. A big distinction between the old and new recording tools is that today the initial attempts at craft for inspiration's sake can be committed to a storage medium. In other words, it is now technically defensible to press the record button at the earliest stage of creation, although it may not be artistically defensible to do so; in fact, it rarely is.

To make a recording is therefore to make two objects: a musical one and a sonic one. The former is assessed in the context of the listener's lifetime exposure to music, in other words, a knowledge- or experienced-based evaluation; the latter is the more objective measure (although there is a subjective component to it). A music recording can be judged as a sonically "good" or "bad" one, regardless of whether the listener is moved by it. Unless it is remarkably good or bad, the sonic object is less relevant than the musical object. Our knowledge of and familiarity with musical sounds modifies their perception. An emotionally affective recording, no matter how poor its technical quality, will be highly regarded by the listener. (Think of how moving Beethoven's Ninth or Barber's Adagio for Strings sounds coming from an old television set. Does it matter that it is low fidelity?)

How will the record be regarded once it is launched into the market's orbit? This is unknowable but it can be considered. An educated guess requires awareness of the competition and musical tastes. Imagine that you operate the only fish sandwich shop in a town where hamburgers are highly valued. It is not necessary that your sandwich be a great one because it is the only product of its type and is not in high demand. Should you opt to sell hamburgers, market pressures will force you make either the greatest or the most readily available sandwich. The best hamburger in a highly competitive market will probably be of a higher caliber than the best fish sandwich. The better acquainted they are with the competition's work and its popularity, the more accurately producers can guess which of their record's qualities will be highly regarded by its buyers. In the studio, producers make choices informed by their stored memory bank of other records. The larger this reservoir, the more production ideas they can draw upon and the easier it is for them to decide which ones are likelier to work.

As the buyer's surrogate, producers' decisions are mindful of who is looking for the product and what he or she will experience upon finding it. There is a crucial difference between wanting something and needing it. Wanting can lead to mere admiration. Needing something is more likely to drive a purchase and is linked to how the listener identifies with the artist and the work. But why do we need music and when do we bond to it? What functions does music serve? Studies of music cognition and social psychology have identified at least seven functions for music: arousal regulation (e.g., to fall asleep; to wake up); coordinating motor activity (e.g., to dance; to exercise); coordinating mental activity (e.g., to focus; to distract); problem solving; emotional regulation; self- and other identification; fantasy. Music lovers recognize their own musical experiences in each of these functions so explanations are unnecessary, but the last four are worth a few words.

Music listening regulates our emotional states by altering the amount of neurotransmitters, such as norepinephrine, serotonin, and dopamine, in the nervous system. It is known that music-induced emotional states are physically and neurochemically identical to emotional states induced by our thoughts or external events. Psychologists have suggested that music may have evolved via the effectiveness with which it can change our moods.

The emotional faculty of empathy allows humans to experience feelings by contagion; we can feel sad about another's problem. Listening to sad songs helps us work out our problems and express strong emotions in a socially safe way. Music, books, movies, and video games let us internally simulate events that substitute for external actions, risky and otherwise. Crying over a sad lyric or movie scene is understandable and accepted by others. When we listen to music we can let a singer take us to the brink of his or her own despair and safely return us minutes later when the song ends. This guided tour of the emotions is especially useful to young people just entering the adult social sphere at an age when reasoned problem solving and emotional regulation can be difficult to untie. It has been said that music lets us don the clothing of the person singing to us. If so, a temporary self can emerge while we identify with lyrics or imagine various social scenes.

Our self-selected social and physical environments reflect our personality, including our music preferences. People prefer music that provides the optimum amount of stimulation at any given time, but this differs broadly among individuals by age, IQ, and personality traits such as extraversion, openness to new experiences, and agreeableness. We bond to our favorite music while sending a message to others about who we are or how we like to be seen. We assume that others' music choices say something about who they are as well. Considering how music functions for the listener, coupled with a realistic sense of who that listener is, helps record makers to select the ideal form for their work.

The more music there is to listen to, the smaller our musical cohort becomes. Today's music marketplace is, all things considered, much larger than ever before and therefore the likelihood of finding others with the same music library as ourselves is rarer. This fact has the potential to make the personal music collection an even better predictor of one's unique personality traits and tastes. The record seller has access to this information, which has ramifications for how products are sold to us.

One final thought on the art of record production concerns the discrepancy between what record makers try to do and what they actually accomplish. While creating a new soup, chefs experiment by tasting and changing it until they are satisfied. They continually measure the distance between what it actually tastes like and their mental image of how they would like it to taste. In this regard, the artist or songwriter is the only one who will ever accurately judge the distance between the intention and the execution of a recorded song. Diners' opinion of the soup is based only on its properties; they haves no idea what it was *supposed to* taste like. Likewise, unless they say so explicitly in an interview, listeners do not know what an artist intended to express; they will interpret the work only through their own frame of reference. This is perhaps the essence of record production—mediating the distance between the artist and the audience. The producer must have the dual sensitivities of understanding what the artist tried to say and to surmise what the listener will actually hear—a necessary and inevitable disparity.

Today's Music Producer

The volume of recorded music is up (in the literal sense of *amount* and in the colloquial sense of *loudness*), but the quality of some codecs has degraded music for those listeners who remember a time when high fidelity was valued. How has that changed the listener's musical experience? Does today's trend of reduced dynamic range (i.e., the use of compressors to increase the apparent overall loudness of individual instruments and their mix) have an impact on how music affects us? The cautious answer is yes. There are affective and anatomical consequences of the so-called loudness war. Dynamic range compression may permit us to listen to music for longer durations, but at the cost of attention to musical and sonic changes that can trigger emotional responses.

Sensory systems have evolved to pay special notice to change to alert us to encroaching threats or opportunities. To preserve neural resources for the business at hand, non-changing signals in our environment are usually ignored. In the auditory modality, newness quickly wears off. Dynamical shifts in the acoustical power of music is used by performers to convey cues about their intentions or the song's meaning. When strong enough to be effective, these changes awaken attentional mechanisms that automatically refresh our focus, alerting us that what is happening is important. To produce a sonic object with no perceptible loudness changes throughout the recording is to focus the listener's attention on the entirety of the piece, rather than on salient points within the piece. It might be argued that in the absence of temporal or melodic changes, this could result in the listener experiencing an overall impression of the artist while missing the subtle and unique aspects of his artistry. The decisions that composers, performers, and producers make to guide the listener's feelings and thoughts can go unnoticed if those details are ultimately packed into a small dynamic space.

Aesthetically, evening out dynamic changes in performance has its place in popular music. Compressors serve to make players sound more consistent, which can increase and maintain the perceived tension in some kinds of music. Styles as diverse as soul and American hardcore derive potency from carefully executed performances that maintain energy at a controlled level throughout the piece—this pregnant tension is rewarded in the release of the final notes. The use of dynamic range compression should be an aesthetic choice for optimizing the chances of an intended emotional outcome. Too often compression is used uncritically, for the purpose of making records sound like everyone else's.

Another potential consequence of reduced dynamic range concerns the amount of time spent listening to music. Without infrequent changes refreshing the attentional system, it is easier to tune out what we are hearing. This is convenient for applied music listening—letting music function as auditory background for working, exercising, driving, and so on. (It is inconvenient for getting your musical message across.) It is less cognitively fatiguing to be constantly reawakened by a stimulus; it follows that the less a signal competes for our attention, the longer we are likely to tolerate it. But whether we attend to it or not does not remove the effect of the stimulus on the sensory organ. The ease with which we can listen to music privately means that more people can be receiving a musical signal for more hours than ever before in human history. Long term exposure to broadband sounds, even at comfortable levels below 70 dB SPL, causes changes both temporary and permanent in the auditory pathway that may desensitize us to sound in the form of hearing loss or hypersensitize us in the form of tinnitus.

Conclusion

So, this discussion may make record production sound very contrived. It is not. What it is is difficult and uncertain. But thoughtful consideration of the work and its aims is the subtext of every casual conversation we have about music, whether we realize it or not. We are exchanging concepts of what music is and learning how it works from others. If we integrate our musical understanding into an understanding of human nature and society, we are better able to make records that function as well-regarded social objects. Here is an example:

Fact: Long intros are boring.

Fact: Because long intros are boring, commercial radio disc jockeys will not play them.

Fact: Geggy Tah's "Whoever You Are" (Luaka Bop, 1996) was a radio hit with a fifty-three-second intro, every second of which was played on major radio stations across the country.

The intro to this recording had a novel amount of complexity and change, allowing it to function as would a song with a short intro. It featured both common and unusual textures and changed through three real or implied time signatures before the opening line. The band's keen sensitivity to where the boundary lay between musical complexity and simplicity allowed it to capture and hold attention for nearly a minute, although in the studio its members were not constructing the intro this deliberately. Awareness of human or musical nature was enough.

Today's music producer is facing new challenges but is armed with many traditional assets. The producer entering the field has far fewer opportunities to produce for record labels or to harness the services of a producer's manager. My former students who are currently making records with unsigned artists have less feedback than I enjoyed or detested from industry professionals. Without the push back from authoritative boundaries, these producer-artists have a more difficult time gauging their own progress. We improve through our failures; not knowing how or if one has failed prevents us from comparing ourselves to the competition, a valuable yardstick of assessment. Working as an independent contractor for an unsigned artist also makes it much harder to navigate the particulars of getting paid, earning royalties, and so on.

Former student Andrew Nault has noted that his clients do not hesitate to write out their checks to engineers but often stall when it comes time to pay producers. (To establish the context, Andrew Nault is extraordinarily talented and his service is in high demand among the local talent.) Is this because producers' contribution makes it seem as though they are part of the band, as though they should be expected to make the same sacrifices in the name of art? Or is it because their contribution—what they actually submit in exchange for their efforts—is so intangible? Engineers hand over files or hard drives in exchange for a check. Producers' contribution is inseparable from the work itself and harder to quantify. Record labels provided a protocol for hiring, firing, and paying their participants, and working outside of this protocol demands that new ground rules be established for every project. This is more difficult when producers have not defined for themselves what they are contributing and how they expect to be compensated for it.

Andrew has what he calls a "gig triangle" for determining whether to sign on for a project. If two of the three points on his triangle are met, he takes the gig. They are: (1) artistry, (2) the professional network, and (3) money. If the record will satisfy his need to develop artistically by solving new musical challenges and expressing critical facets of his creativity, it meets his need for artistic growth. If the record will help him gain exposure in the music industry, it meets his need for professional growth. If it pays, it meets his need to make records for a living. When I worked in the music industry, this last point was always there; I only had to consider the other two. The young producers who make records in the current market will build their careers on willpower, sacrifice, and passion. Those are undeniably strong assets for creating art but they can be short-lived without the traditional rewards of money and recognition.

Building one's own momentum is how great careers are launched. This generation of producers is just as passionate and committed as was the previous generation. They have little choice but to be self-starting and to be prepared to sustain themselves for an indefinite time. Today's technology permits the opportunity to build a long résumé despite never having been paid by a record label. Strictly speaking, it allows there to be more "recording artists" than ever before, and this means more potential work in one's own backyard. The growth of regional music scenes is driven by the shrinking national music scene; as noted, listeners have more music to choose from and therefore the music they consume can be more reflective of their own environment. It is hoped that this will encourage young producers to work within their community and to build their own sound as inextricably part of a regional sound. If the resources are there to sustain this scenario, record making will develop in the most exciting way that it can—from the seeds of reinvention. In this light, *what* producers think (and by extension, what tools they use) is subordinate to *how* they think.

The Death of Music

by EUGENE S. ROBINSON

The scales have fallen from my eyes; it's more dire than people think. The labels know nothing, care about nothing, not even apparently, cash; the bands are willing to go along with these know-nothings; and the ill-informed public would be more than happy to listen to nothing but commercial jingles for the rest of forever. And the guys who are in a position to help—those so-called who have "made it"—are so stunned that they have made it that they can't be bothered to do much other than count their cash, what little is left, and get high. A reasonable response in many ways but not one that will service the muse of musical art, standard bearing all of our secret desires loudly and through Marshall amps.

But we get ahead of ourselves here and doing so runs the perilous risk (to us, at least) of diagnosing the patient's illness by starting with a critique of his garden's floral pattern. The issue, as far as we've been able to articulate it, has everything to do with the song's evolving from becoming to being. In a strict sense this is a very short and simple journey: Moved by the idea of a song, perhaps the Platonic triad or just a burst of sudden musical joy, musical noise will leave the agent's mouth and newly populate the world with the artist's idea, made real with music, of the exact parameters of their place in space. A joyous song. A sad song. A song of ineffable yearning.

You sing it. I hear it. The circle is squared and we've captured the long and short of an experience. And this works. Until I want to hear it again. At that point I compel you to sing it again (through cajoling or perhaps the force of arms, if things get out of hand), but am disturbed to find out that this song sung on this other day does nothing for me. It is a different song.

Flash forward to now and what you have is an entire industry bent on capturing the original song, as it is first sprung forth from the egg.

Our documentation of our culture is our culture. And things don't get any easier from here: what we use, to capture the first blush of the simple joy of song, is now an industry and a technology. Yes, it spares the singer the onus of having to come to all of our houses, one by one, to sing "Hey Jude," but it also jams your orange full of clockwork parts until whatever is remembered of the original burst of Eros that is music is a memory of a memory of something someone else had said to someone when you were not around. And the tools used to create this stuff—is the biggest scam of it all, 90 percent of the time, as it actually degrades the actual experience while propping up its faux variant. By this measure it has to be said that selling the real fake is much better than selling the fake fake.

And yes, if Auto-Tune, a software program that can make a singer out of Anthony Kiedis can, um, actually make a song out of Anthony Kiedis's singing, is this so wrong? Are we Luddites?

This is all philosophical clothes washing that could go on for hours and provide ample justification for having yet another glass of wine *if* the technology had not made it so simple for the industry to destroy itself, and very possibly, the entire machinery of music making. No one, not even a Stalin, can stop the singing (though it is curious that totalitarian governments are responsible for so little serious musical culture). But twenty million kids with computers might stop the documentation of it. Which is to say, stop the creation of culture. Or rather, the creation of culture via an industry that documents and financially *remunerates* the documentarians.

Would the Sex Pistols' music have been any better if they all had had to maintain day jobs? Forever?

And were artists really getting remunerated properly? And if everything is stolen, and the songs of the future are simply songs sung by someone who was moved by the muse to do so, aren't we approaching a return to Year Zero? Is light at the end of the tunnel? That is: as distribution gets more democratic it becomes easier to end run around the sinkhole of Hollywood, right? The self-same industry that turned the Doors into a nice, comfortable package maybe should be written out of the community equation in regards to music making, yes? I mean, a record exec's getting a Ferrari will not in any way make us like Britney Spears more. So, is it not genuinely an improvement, this death of the musical apparatus as it stands: large recording studios, large record labels, large salaries, large egos?

Suuuurrre...look, you can rest assured that Hollywood will extract its pound of flesh, one way or another (because no one likes to give money back), *and* in all likelihood, after pulling its fat from the fire will indubitably throw it right back in again. Because we eat ourselves. But maybe this is unnecessarily paranoid. Maybe it's not so much a willing consumption of self and its standard bearing of the ethos of Eros but more a kind of gross egoism. The same one that caused Vic Morrow to say in the classic juvenile delinquent film of the '50s, "You have *never* been my age, Pops."

Of course the flip side of this adolescent coin is a cynicism that makes getting out of bed difficult and that's that: we *have* all been that age, sonny. And the vast collection of human culture is a culture of collective amnesia. Which is all well and good. Maybe even better that we forget everything every two decades. It keeps us creating. However, if we had forgotten how to rotate crops, we'd all be eating dust and so again: the repackaging of the old as the new and the continued consumption of the same is the engine that drives this great big machine of modernity.

Which is my way of saying that I think we have nothing to worry about: as long as we have mouths.

Why "Strawberry Fields Forever" Matters

by BOBBY FRASIER

Music is a fickle mistress. Quite elusive, actually. As a consumer, you buy music (at least you should), but you don't buy music. You buy the right to play back a given medium with information on the disc, tape, or three-dimensional holographic magnetic bubble memory, et al, that correlates to a given playback system, which then translates the given medium, in most cases electronically, to be sent to a transduction system to enable vibrations to be created in the air, thereby inducing a response in another transduction mechanism, with its beginnings located on the side of the human head and ending as synaptic response in the brain. This entire process then produces an emotional response. The response runs the gamut of the human experience: said transduction could make you wanna move, make you wanna groove, or could induce high levels of tension, resulting in "make you wanna puke." Quite a responsibility for content providers, no?

Some may say that that is exactly correct: the answer is a resounding no. The artist lacks any and all responsibility as it pertains to exactly how another human reacts to his or her creation. How could an artist *possibly* take into account every person's reaction to sound? Of course, it can't be done, because each individual's response is unique. To quote a particularly notable musician/artist/poet/writer/actor of the twentieth century, John Lennon:

> My role in society, or any artist's or poet's role, is to try and express what we all feel. Not to tell people how to feel. Not as a preacher, not as a leader, but as a reflection of us all.

This, to me, expresses successful composition; the universality of creation, the common bond. Granted, not everyone is going to have the same experience to pull from when it comes to contemplation of an artist's vision. As an example, I did not grow up in an inner-city environment or in poverty. Certain genres of music address this experience to which I simply do not relate. I understand, intellectually, the travails and plight, but I am unable to access an emotional response due to the lack of a truly empirical experience. I have a compassionate response, but for me personally (and I might as well refer to these genres by name), rap music does not stir my soul. In like kind, the traditional music of India may not stir the soul of the person growing up in Franklin, Tennessee, where the genre of American country music could have been the norm of his or her formative years.

This heralds the all-imposing "elephant-in-the-room" question: What are the qualifying parameters that dictate a human's response to music? Is it generational, with each generation justifying *its* music as being the greatest music ever written? Is it situational, with music being the background of our defining moments in life? Or is it, as author Daniel J. Levitin argues, that music is a fundamental aspect of our species, possibly even more than language? An evaluation of all of these aspects would indicate the answer to lie within a bit of each of these questions. I defer to Mr. Levitin and his book *This Is Your Brain on Music: The Science of a Human Obsession* (Dutton, 2006) for a thoroughly delightful study addressing these very questions. For me, as a musician, educator, audio recorder, performer, and writer, I simply have to ascertain a consensus, based on my own experience, as we all do, and come to conclusions based on my own observations.

My formative years were inundated with musical genres. When we're young, we listen to what is around us, what our parents, brothers, and sisters listen to. I heard rock and roll from Elvis and Ricky Nelson, classical music (Holst seemed to be a favorite around age four), and many varied performances from television, in particular, through variety shows of the day, such as *The Ed Sullivan Show*. But more than any other genre, country-western music was the music of my parents. So, for me, it was Patsy Cline, Jim Reeves, Charlie

Pride, Buck Owens, Hank Williams, et al, in the late 1950s and early '60s. I also listened to children's records, of course. One in particular "struck me" (pun intended) quite hard—it was called "El Kabong!" For those of you studied in the world of historical cartoons, El Kabong was the masked vigilante alter-ego of one cartoon horse by the name of Quick Draw McGraw. The sound made by the weapon of choice, a guitar, as it struck its intended victim, was what attracted me to the guitar somewhere around the age of three or four. It was at that time that I made the decision to become a guitarist. Many of my peers, who have heard me play, will attest that I am still attempting to capture the sound of a crashing, out-of-tune guitar during any given performance. Early influences loom large in our consciousness.

Given the reference to my musical upbringing, one might have expected me to lean heavily toward "country." As with many children, however, a rebellion took place regarding the music of my parents. In the early 1960s this equated to "surf music," coming from the Beach Boys and the duo of Jan & Dean, which was basically rock and roll redux. And, as the title of this treatise dictates, another influence shadowed the power of all previous stirrings of the soul.

I had "heard of them," but don't really recall "hearing them" on TV or the radio. But I knew they were coming. Everybody knew they were coming. I was seven years old; I wasn't quite locked into current events and the collective consciousness of society like the Internet-surfing, iPhone-toting, online-social-networking seven-year-old of the twenty-first century (insert the current technology of the day when you're reading this).

The Beatles' appearance on *The Ed Sullivan Show* on February 9, 1964, has been heralded as an official Earth-Altering-Event. Not by me (well, *yes*, by me), but by the thousands upon thousands upon thousands of words printed in magazines, newspapers, books, and on websites. The phenomenon continues. There continue to be new books, new materials, new interviews, new studies, new music, appearing on a regular basis. Movies, a Las Vegas show, bootlegs . . . Still, as of this writing, there is a craving for more. Why?

Speaking strictly from the first person, for me, the Beatles got into my DNA and never left. The timeless melodies, clever musical arrangements and wordings, voicings of the guitar parts, the perfectly balanced production techniques of Sir George Martin—all arrived at the same point at the same time. This was a confluence of energies; call it an alignment of the stars, if you will. Perhaps, if any one element of the Beatles Phenomenon had been changed, an entirely different outcome could have taken place. It didn't, and their music stands as a body of work that encourages, influences, and inspires writers, performers, musicians, producers, and engineers, today, and one hopes, for all eternity.

I enjoy other types of music. But the Beatles are Rock and Roll 201, the meat of the subject material. They brought Rock and Roll 101 (Bill Haley, Elvis Presley, Chuck Berry, Big Joe Turner, Fats Domino, Little Richard, etc.) to an entirely new generation, people who had not heard nor grown up with it. Yes, at age seven, I thought "Rock and Roll Music" and "Roll Over Beethoven" were songs written by the Beatles. I didn't care—the point is that they brought *the feeling* along with them, and gave it their own.

I consider Rock and Roll 102 to be the rearrangement of early rock and roll, the unusually dark period from the late '50s into the early '60s, characterized by much corporate doo-wop and general sappiness, and not much inspiration. I speak in generalities here because, as in any era, there are gems amongst the coal. If you look at what was on the charts at the time of the Beatles' arrival, historically, you can certainly see (and hear) the massive paradigm shift that their music, and performance, entailed. There was nothing like them. And I don't believe there shall ever be a phenomenon like them again. Not in my lifetime. I am waiting, and I will certainly acknowledge the second coming as such. You can catch me on YouTube, dancing in the streets.

Now, with that said, those who were teens during the "Dark Ages" may disagree with me. Bobby Darin's "Beyond the Sea" from 1959 may hold the same place in their hearts that "Oh! Darling," from the Beatles' *Abbey Road* LP, does for me. This reflects one of the questions put forth at the beginning of this diatribe: are the power and meaning of music generational?

I put this question to you, the reader: Is the music that is being marketed to the youth of America (and the world), at the time you are reading this, timeless enough to make a comeback, forty to fifty years from its inception as "pop music"? Will Kanye West have an entire stadium built just for presentation of his music, and its interpretation by another art form (say, acrobatics...), forty years after its release date? If Mr. West is indeed the "voice of his generation" as he has claimed, then I say yes. His music will be etched into the very fiber of the listener's being, forever moving the soul in an inexplicable fashion, exactly as the Beatles' did for me. You can insert any pop artist of the day in place of Mr. West, to your liking.

The music that plays behind the story of your life will always have a particular meaning to *you*. But timeless art—the renaissance, if you will—doesn't happen every ten years. And it is this concept, this prime directive, which informs my contribution to the body of work you have in your hand (or on your computer—or your cerebral-opto implants...) through exploration of why "Strawberry Fields Forever" matters.

> "The Beatles took the world from black-and-white into color." —Martin Scorsese, introduction to the 2007 DVD rerelease of the movie, *Help!*

The 1960s, and particularly the Beatles' contributions to that decade, was without a doubt, *the* era of discovery in the world of pop music and the recording techniques thereof. New innovations were taking place, technologically, musically, socially, and politically. As I've stated before, the convolution of personalities all converged to create an atmosphere of forward movement. Nobody wrote like the Beatles, nobody *sounded* like the Beatles, and this was in no small part attributable to the contributions of their engineers, Norman Smith and Geoff Emerick (to name the major figures), and producer George Martin. Innovation: let's try it. By today's standards, the Beatles were using stone knives and bearskins to make records. Yet why do these records, sonically and musically, still stand up to today's scrutiny?

I am an instructor at a school for audio recording. We have tools that are light-years beyond what was being employed at EMI studios in the 1960s. Every artist, every producer, every kid with a desktop computer (or even a mobile phone) has the ability to create music today. The democratization of production has become so widespread that one would think, "Wow, there is more opportunity today, for more people to be making great music. And, statistically speaking *alone*, there should be more great music out there!" Why am I not hearing it?

Marketing is one big deciding factor in the equation. Sell what sells. Find the formula and beat it into the ground. Despite the risk of being held in the low-esteem position of aging flatulence, I nonetheless conclude that what I hear on the "airwaves" (traditional radio, satellite radio, television, cable, Internet) is redundant. "Who is that?" I'll ask my wife, children, friends, or students. And sometimes they will know. Most times, however, I receive the "It sounds like [insert other band here]" reply. There is an incredible sameness that permeates the land. This is exactly my response to "rap music." Please, give me something I haven't heard before. The repetition of rap does not stir my soul. Not from the lack of common experience, as mentioned previously, but from the redundancy of the music. It's not interesting. I've already heard that one handclap from that one drum machine. Please, do something original.

Originality *is* out there, and sometimes it hits. But I don't see a body of work being published by any one artist, or group of artists, that constitutes the same consistency and innovation that was put forth by the Beatles. They are the benchmark.

This is why "Strawberry Fields Forever" matters: It was the first song to be recorded after the Beatles' decision to stop touring in late 1966. A conscious decision was made to create music that couldn't be played live. Prior to this, they wrote songs to add to their set list. With the release of *Revolver* on August 5, 1966, it was already apparent that the songs "Tomorrow Never Knows," "Eleanor Rigby," and "Got to Get You into My Life," were not going to be on the set list; they were orchestrated and experimental. Yet "Strawberry Fields Forever" was the true turning point, a moment in musical history that said, "The recording studio is now an instrument unto itself."

This is why "Strawberry Fields Forever" matters: It took forty-five hours, over a period of five weeks, to record the song. the Beatles' first complete LP record, *Please Please Me*, was recorded in one day: nine hours and forty-five minutes, to be exact. "Strawberry Fields Forever" was not only technically pushing the boundaries of audio recording, but also the realms of poetic license. Lennon was said to describe the song as "psychoanalysis set to music." But, as has already been reported, his belief was that a poet should "try and express what we all feel." Each individual takes something different away from this song. For me, that is the true test of great songwriting. The song is so universal that each individual has an experience that can correlate with the ambiguity. Ambiguous yet poignant, simultaneously. Carl Jung referred extensively to the "tension of opposites." The Beatles were masters at this, not only in words, but in the feel of their music as well.

This is why "Strawberry Fields Forever" matters: Using a 4-track tape recorder, and the talents of engineer Geoff Emerick and producer George Martin, the song was a sojourn through the gates of tinkering. An entire dissertation could be constructed at this point on how it was arranged, rearranged, rerecorded, orchestrated, and edited, but I will leave the reader to research this methodology. What I find fascinating is the speed at which they worked. Today, we have virtually limitless track count, unfathomable editing and tuning capabilities, and this very embodiment of choices allows some projects to trudge on for what seems like an eternity. As I tell my students, talent in front of the microphone makes *our* job *much* easier.

Which is why "Strawberry Fields Forever" matters. The element of discovery, using, by today's standards, primitive tools, and a constant search for new meaning, new art, new sounds, new directions: this was the driving force behind the

Beatles. We live in the age of assembly, with much less discovery taking place. But, a renaissance doesn't happen every ten years... When I do hear something unusual, something that sounds different, and stirs my soul, my musical passion, I simply must find it. The advent of programs such as Shazam for the iPhone are making this search become reality. Finding the music is more than half the battle, and this is just for music that I happen to be hearing at the moment, on TV, in a restaurant, or at a shopping mall. What about the music that *isn't* getting widespread airplay? That's another topic entirely, searching through the noise to find the melody...

Each generation and decade has a sound or timbre. It is created through many factors: the technology available at the time, the stylization of the music, the instrumentation, the orchestration, and, perhaps, a collective consciousness of "where the music should be going." Music of the '30s, '40s, and '50s all sounds distinctive because of the technology of recording. And, of course, you could say the same of music in the era of acoustic recording, prior to microphones and electronics. (Everything's going back to wax, you know...) Each decade has a sound. The 1980s were awash with reverb, due to the new digital technologies that *had* to be overused, mostly due to the cost of the units. (If you paid twelve thousand dollars for a reverb in 1979, you'd want to use it—on *everything*.) With the advent of drum machines, MIDI programming, and inexpensive sound synthesis, the '80s had a *sound* about it. The Solid State Logic mixing console introduced in 1977 became the de facto standard for mixing hit records. It has a compressor on every channel, plus a master bus compressor. Most hit records were recorded using this mixing desk, another commonality in the sound of the 1980s.

Today we have software, and lots of it. Auto-Tune programming has become a phrase known by the layman; it is truly etched into the lexicon of our society. (I recently read an entire article about the technology in a local, conservative newspaper—you remember newspapers, don't you?) When I hear someone say, "That's been Auto-Tuned," then I know the effect is not only being overused, it has become a known part of the sound of the music. It's one thing to be hit in the face with the "Cher effect," named for that artist's 1998 release "Believe." Within that song an obvious effect was happening, one of the first uses of the Auto-Tune process. But when the vocal tracks are much more subtly processed and people are noticing the sound of the effect itself, it seems obvious to me that the sound of the process has now become part of the very fabric of the music. The repetitive use fuels an expectation of the modern production characteristic. The discography of T-Pain is a more current example of Auto-Tune used as an effect (or, some may say, a gimmick) creating the "signature sound" of this particular artist.

We have the ability to perfect our music. Today's listener demands it, because that's what they've been hearing for the last ten years (as of this writing). Every vocal is processed to the point of its virtually being a different instrument. Much of the "life" of a vocalist is now relegated to the editing bin, to be processed, tuned, compressed, and turned into a synthetic sound. Compressors (an electronic device that limits the dynamic range of an electronic signal) are used to increase volume levels to unlistenable limits. This form of production simply cannot be sustained. It will not endure the test of time. The legacy of the 2000s will be: "overcompressed, overtuned, and too loud." Just as in rap, I find the repetition of production as irritating as the repetition of music. But by perfecting the music, isn't that act unto itself, removing the perfection that is the human performance?

This is why "Strawberry Fields Forever" matters. There was no Auto-Tune, there were no unlimited track counts, there were no virtual instruments. Just stone knives and bearskins and a desire to create an artistic statement that no one had ever heard before.

The audio recording school where I'm employed deals with postsecondary adult education. The average age of a student is around nineteen years old. I hear all kinds of music from the students, as their tastes vary, but for the most part it falls into five categories: rap/hip-hop, R&B, death/black/speed metal, country-western, and experimental. (I'm going to put jazz and flamboyant-chops music in the experimental category, because I hear so very little of either.)

I'm often asked to listen to something, usually the work of a group the student really, really likes. In the six years I've been teaching (as of this writing), I haven't heard one single thing that a student brings me that I find interesting. Really. Now, is this generational, or are they simply listening to crap because their parents don't like it? I've inquired, as in, "How do you feel about this music—how does it make you feel?" and I usually get some variation of, "This is the s--t." What does that mean? "It's just the s--t, man. Don't you get it?"

Apparently not. Most of what I hear does not resonate with my particular being. Yet, I find many, many students who are fascinated and absolutely fanatical about the music of the Beatles. And for those students who have *never* heard the music of the Beatles (I have had many students who have never heard the music of the Beatles, and I equate this to someone who enters art school never having seen a Picasso, Rembrandt, or Monet...) usually, after one listening session, they are humming the melodies. Ah, those infectious melodies. A lost art? In some genres, yes. Give me something new; nobody goes away humming the kick drum.

Which is why "Strawberry Fields Forever" matters. How you gonna know where you're goin' if ya don't know where you been?

Modern Recording Fidelity and the Digital Download World

by ADAM AYAN

Modern recording technology is as sophisticated and diverse as ever, possibly the best it has ever been. The combination of high-end analog technology and the best digital recording technology ever available affords recording professionals the tools to best express music as a recorded art. However, one could make the argument that we as an industry seem to be underutilizing the tools at our disposal. Why is this?

As a mastering engineer in the recording industry, I am fortunate enough to work on some really fantastic music and recordings. Be it rock, pop, metal, country, or jazz, my job is always the same: master to best convey my clients' recordings to the listener. In short, make it sound great, nothing less than perfection.

I began my career at a very interesting time in the recording industry, a time of major changes in the way music is both created and "consumed." The late 1990s and early 2000s saw a boom in digital recording technology and, specifically, the ability to record multitrack on a computer/digital audio workstation (DAW). Around that same time we also saw the rise of peer-to-peer networks, where illegal music file sharing flourished, and then eventually the creation of successful and legitimate digital download sites such as Apple's iTunes.

I started my professional audio/engineering career in 1996 at the age of twenty-one. At the time I was a senior at the University of Massachusetts at Lowell, enrolled as an undergraduate student majoring in music performance/sound recording technology. Academically, I was working in the SRT program's 2-inch, 24-track all-analog studio, recording my final multitrack project before graduation. Simultaneously, I was working professionally as an assistant at a digital multitrack studio in southern New Hampshire, near the UMass Lowell campus. West Sound Studios was the name of the place, and we ran thirty-two digital tracks of Tascam DA-88s (four 8-channel machines running in sync) with a Yamaha 02R digital console with automation (!). It was the cutting edge of project studio digital technology. Many larger commercial facilities were still recording to 2-inch analog tape at that time, a format that always seemed out of reach (financially and logistically) for any smaller project studio. At West Sound we were mixing to DAT, and doing final editing of our DAT mixes loaded into Sound Designer software on a Mac. Editing stereo audio in the computer was pretty cool and relatively new, at least in the recording/project studio world. I remember a time, working at West Sound, when the studio began seriously considering a leap to Digidesign's Pro Tools DAW, not only for editing, but for multitrack recording and mixing. This was a big deal! Then, many studios were still recording to 2-inch tape in the analog world, or a variety of tape-based digital multitrack formats (such as those Tascam DA-88s). Recording and mixing on a hard drive was still a novel idea, whose time was coming right around the corner.

By 1997 I had graduated from the program at UMass Lowell, and in August 1998 I found myself with a dream job as a production engineer at Gateway Mastering Studios in Portland, Maine (where I work to this day as a mastering engineer!). I cut production masters on Sony's 1630 format, and on audio CD. I did digital editing on a Sonic Solutions DAW, of which we had four at the time, networked together using Sonic's MediaNet system. Very cutting edge! With the MediaNet you could playback, record, and edit audio over a computer network. At that time, virtually all world-class mastering studios in the United States were running Sonic Solutions as their DAW of choice and making most masters on 1630. If you were proficient at both, and had great ears for quality control, you were able to perform the duties of a production engineer.

The presence of digital audio workstations in the recording and mixing studios was just starting to become commonplace.

Until then, a lot of the final digital editing was being done at the mastering studio, on the Sonic Solutions system. Most recording studios that did have DAWs used them for final stereo editing, but not so much for multitrack recording and mixing yet.

By the end of the '90s and early 2000s, almost every recording studio in the States had a multitrack DAW (mostly Digidesign's Pro Tools), used to record and mix. The analog 2-inch was also available and still used a fair amount. It wasn't very long before that changed. I visited several world-class recording studios in Nashville in the spring of 2003. At every studio I heard the same thing: the 2-inch machine was hardly ever used anymore. Almost everybody was recording straight into the DAW. In fact, virtually all artists were recording into the DAW, then bringing their hard drive home to record overdubs and edit on their own system, then (hopefully) coming back to the world-class facility for the final mix. This was not unique to the Nashville recording community, it was beginning to happen everywhere.

Once multitrack recording on a digital audio workstation became a true possibility, everything began to change, for good and bad. It not only became affordable to build your own studio and record at home (*and* possibly achieve professional quality and results), it became even less expensive than working at a commercial recording studio. It became possible to easily move from one recording space to another, as Pro Tools became the de facto "standard" DAW. Record drums and bass at one studio, then bring your FireWire or USB (or

SCSI, early on) hard drive to another to record your guitar and vocal overdubs. Send your files to a friend on the other side of country (or world!) to add more parts, and do it over the Internet if you'd like. The possibilities are fantastic!

There was also an explosion in new, high-resolution digital formats as well. All of the DAWs were able to record, edit, and play back at 24-bit depth resolution (much better than those old 16-bit DATs), and soon many of them would also record at higher sampling rates, 88.2 kHz, 96 kHz, 176.4 kHz, and 192 kHz. There were also new consumer formats that were able to deliver high-resolution digital audio to the listener; both the DVD-Audio and SACD (Super Audio CD) formats came on the market—and both were initially touted as the future replacement of the audio CD.

Recording professionals and musicians alike now have a myriad of high-quality choices when making a record. Artists, producers, or engineers may like to record some (if not all tracks) to 2–inch analog tape, then transfer into the DAW for final overdubs, editing, and mixing. They may also prefer the sound of mixing to ½-inch or 1-inch tape, as opposed to digital. Record some or most tracks on analog if that's what you like, then record overdubs on the DAW, edit in the DAW, and mix down to analog again. Why not? You can have the best of both worlds (analog and digital), and choose your recording tools and techniques based on the sounds most conducive to the music you make.

In my mastering studio at Gateway Mastering, I have a good mix of both digital and analog tools. All the best/most sophisticated mastering equalizers, compressors, and limiters. I find that I generally like using a "hybrid" signal path (both analog and digital), even when presented with a digital mix. Basically, it's about the tools, and sonic options. Digital to analog converters (and analog-to-digital converters) have become so good, that moving from digital to analog (and vice versa) has become as sonically transparent as ever. Arguments and debates over what is better, analog or digital, continue, yet to a much lesser degree than ever. Digital audio technology has gotten so good that many do not find any compromises when working in the digital domain. In my opinion, we as recording professionals have many tools at our disposal, and can mix and match them if we'd like. All-analog may or may not be the way to go for a particular recording project (take it all the way to vinyl if that's your thing!). All-digital may or may not be the way to go. A combination of analog and digital may be the proper route, as long as you achieve your sonic goals.

With all of these new possibilities in the world of recording, why do we feel—more than ever—that we may have to make compromises in the way we make our music, and the way consumers listen to it?

Unfortunately, the new high-resolution digital consumer formats introduced in the early 2000s did not flourish, and both DVD-Audio and the SACD formats were abandoned by the major record labels in the United States. Neither format became the higher-quality replacement for the audio CD. I believe that the consumer spoke, and preferred relatively inexpensive (and lesser-quality) digital downloads over new higher-resolution disc-based formats.

So, is it the way people "consume" music that is to blame? Most of today's music fans are not sitting in their living room, in the listening "sweet spot" of the stereo field, taking in every note of their favorite artist's new album. Most fans are listening in their car, on their laptop, or to their iPod with earbuds. And in most of these cases, the car, the living room, and so on, the listening device is most likely the iPod or some other portable device equivalent.

Portability has certainly superseded fidelity for most modern music consumers. In the 1980s, when I was a young fan of music and a musician myself, my listening device of choice was the Sony Walkman. I loved the fact that I could walk to school and listen to my favorite music. I could bring it anywhere. The sonic quality of cassettes was certainly inferior to vinyl and CDs, but I didn't care. Portability trumped fidelity for me at the time. The ability to make my own mix tapes and listen to them anywhere was awesome! As I discovered the power a great recording has to convey a musical message, I opted for higher fidelity, but I can understand the consumer's preference for portability. The good news is that cassettes were inferior in sound quality to the MP3s (most of the time!) and AAC files used in today's portable devices. So . . . we have made a few steps forward in terms of consumer portability and fidelity. Yet, in the past decade, we have taken a few steps back in overall quality (from CD quality to MP3s, etc.) and arguably a step back in terms of overall production quality.

According to a *New York Times* article published in late 2008:

> Total album sales in the United States, including CDs and full-album downloads, were 428 million, a 14 percent drop from 2007, according to data from Nielsen SoundScan. Since the industry's peak in 2000, album sales have declined 45 percent, although digital music purchases continue to grow at a rapid rate. Sales of digital music continued to rise steeply last year. Just over a billion songs were downloaded, a 27 percent increase from 2007, and some record companies say they are finally beginning to wring significant profits from music on Web sites like YouTube and MySpace. But analysts say that despite the growth and promise of digital music—in 2003 just 19 million songs were purchased as downloads—the money made online is still far from enough to make up for losses in physical sales.

Due to this trend of decline in music sales, today's record production budgets are smaller than ever in almost all cases. Sales of recorded music on a whole are down. The numbers for 2008 show a major decline for physical media (CDs) and full album sales, and an increase in digital download sales of single songs. And the increase in single song sales does not make up for the decline in album sales. So, there is less capital to be invested in music production. Legendary world-class recording facilities (with unparalleled acoustic environments) have gone out of business, and musicians are recording at home. In some cases, the latter are recording tracks without the help of an audio/recording professional. The affordability and flexibility of home recording is fantastic, but in some cases (certainly not all!) it has made it more difficult to make amazing-sounding recordings. The big rooms of world-class places, with their great acoustics, are underutilized, if utilized at all. More often than not, artistic compromises are made, and records are recorded and mixed in less than perfect environments.

Shrinking recording budgets, a direct effect of the decline in album/music/CD sales, have had a major impact on how we make our music. Producers, recording engineers, and artists are being asked to do a lot more with a lot less (money and time!), and to do it in new environments. Many of my clients, who are producers and engineers, have told me they find it impossible to function within the current budget limitations without having their own studio in which to work. Many of them have a Pro Tools–based studio at home, and they may still work in commercial facilities—but not all of the time. They are working in recording environments that are not what they consider ideal, but because they are exceptionally good at what they do, they have adapted and continue to do great work. If asked, however, they would most likely prefer to work in world-class studios, equipped with great rooms and great acoustic spaces.

There are, of course, upsides to working in the DAW and working at your own studio. There isn't the pressure to watch the clock, knowing that valuable studio time is passing. There is also the luxury of recording whenever the moment strikes you and the artist, capturing special musical moments that might otherwise have been missed.... Full automated recall of an "in the box" (all-DAW) mix makes minor revisions and changes cost effective and viable.

The short of it is, compromises may be made to stay within budget and on deadline. Instead of having the ability to utilize all recording possibilities, recording professionals are bound to what is financially feasible in a shrinking market. This does not always bode well for the musical perfectionist in all of us!

The good news is that music consumers do want to purchase music (as opposed to pirating it!); the growth in digital download sales is proof. The even better news for audio fidelity is the proliferation of high-speed Internet access, as well as the growth of large-capacity data storage, both for computers and listening devices such as the iPod. As of January 2009, Apple announced that all of the four major record labels would be offering their music as 256 kbps AAC files, a higher bit rate twice that of the previous norm (128 kbps) at the iTunes Music Store (www.apple.com/pr/library/2009/01/06itunes. html). Many artists have also made even higher resolution downloads available through their own websites, from CD-quality files (44.1 kHz/16-bit) to 96 kHz/24-bit. This is a glimmer of hope for higher-fidelity downloadable purchases in the future. If consumers place value in them, and are willing to pay for them, this will create an upswing in sales for the music industry, and one may hope, an increase in budgets for future music recordings.

from the ability to distribute, market, and sell their own product cheaply, which in turn empowers us, the consumer, who is tapped into the same pipeline. Recording artist and free musical market pioneer Ani DiFranco figured this out in 1989 when she started her own label, turning down lucrative offers from record companies. Ms. DiFranco provided a wake-up call for an industry that had no idea what was coming. This is remarkable, as she took this leap without the Internet.

The net is the factor that brought this all together by giving artists the tools necessary to sell their product. How it all works was artfully put forth by author and *Wired* editor Chris Anderson in his book *The Long Tail* (Hyperion, 2006). The theory described in his book has broad applications but it applies best here by explaining how new order Internet businesses such as Sweetwater, iTunes, and Amazon can sell a huge range of products in small quantities. Volume sales is nothing new, but in our world, adding together the ability to produce music cheaply, then market and manage the sale of that product on the Internet, is the hat trick that enables the artist to maintain control of their art and make a living.

A look at typical search engine results shows how the tail works. According to Anderson, if you break down Internet searches of [place category here], the top 100 hits account for 6 percent of traffic, the top 500 come in at 9 percent, the top 1,000 at 11 percent, and the top 10,000 at 19 percent. The point being that the majority of action is in the tail. For music, this means that an artist who is not Top 10, 100, or even 5,000 has sales potential because the consumer has access to a "store" that's a million miles wide and 1 inch deep. Granted, it's not the kind of dollars a "hit" would generate—millions of copies sold at great profit. But that model is only realistic for the very few artists breathing the rarified air at the top of the pyramid.

How do you find all this great music I referred to in point three, along the daunting and massive tail? One method was inadvertently demonstrated to me at a restaurant. While waiting for my food, I observed other patrons listening to the music piped in through the ceiling speakers. Two girls in their late twenties were eating a few tables away, and seated a few tables from them were a mother in her thirties and her five-year-old daughter. A song came on the in-house system which I'd never heard before. The twenty-somethings were mouthing along the words of this song, and a minute later, the five-year-old said to her mom, "I like that song." I'd never heard this particular track but was curious what artist could move both a five-year-old and someone twenty years older.

This is where some "sticky" tech came into play. I have an iPhone and a lot of free apps, including Shazam, a one-trick pony that can "listen" to a track through the phone's speaker and "tag" it. By tagging the track, Shazam gives you the artist bio/discography, album name, label, date it was tagged, and where to buy it online. I opened Shazam, set my phone on the table, and within two minutes I found the tune: Matt Nathanson's "Come on Get Higher" from the album *Some Mad Hope*. I did some research and found that Matt is a San

Francisco–based artist who released four independent titles between 1993 and 1999. He was signed to Universal and released *Beneath These Fireworks* in 2003 and *Some Mad Hope* in 2007. The CD I tagged was ranked #706 on Amazon. com, with Matt's other titles ranking well out into the tail. Matt has spanned the gap between old and new models by being signed to a traditional label but still remaining viable by releasing his own product and supporting himself through touring.

Another example I found is Pomplamoose, a Bay Area duo whose music is marketed and sold entirely within the tail. Pomplamoose is comprised of Nataly Dawn and Jack Conte, who produce their own recordings and get the word out via craftily edited videos on their YouTube channel (pomplamoosemusic) and sell their downloads on MySpace and iTunes for ninety-nine cents. Web hits for video covers of "My Favorite Things," "La Vie en Rose," and other well-written catchy originals with great lyrics range from thirty thousand to ten times that. They've gone viral on their own without a record company and the "old world" of traditional TV advertising is buying in. Their cover of "Mr. Sandman" was recently used by Toyota as background music for a '50s-themed Avalon commercial and they've got covers of "Jingle Bells" and "Up on the Housetop," plus themselves in two holiday-themed Hyundai commercials shot in the style of their YouTube videos.

My "finds" are but a small example of the viral power of the Internet and how things will be. Malcolm Gladwell talks about how products become epidemic in his book *The Tipping Point* (Little, Brown, 2000), but it is more quickly explained by the behavior of killer bees. How does their lethal conduct go viral? The first bee that stings an intruder releases a pheromone that alerts the next bee that this is an enemy worth giving its life for, who releases its "tag" for the next bee, and so on. This is the nature of the Internet and how things get exponentially noticed and sold.

So what's next? For me, the consumer's love of lo-fi is a drag, but I believe quality will be resurgent. As an educator I see it all the time—when I play a great recording on a great system for students, the light goes on and they "get it." When quality becomes cheap and easy to deliver, people will buy it and be on board in a big way.

There will be new mobile apps and social networks to help sift through the dross of the tail and get to the good stuff. We'll be able to zero in and buy à la carte, and while the residents of the tail won't get rich, they will be able to support themselves and keep creating real music and art.

For now, we've all got to do our own work to seek out great music. If you can't find it, you're looking in the wrong place. Radio as we've known it, big-hit artists, CDs and DVDs, nonvinyl record stores, and traditional sales models have moved into the cutout bin and have been supplanted by the Internet. Is there crap out there? Oh, *yes*! But that's life in the tail, and life is good. As consumers, we've got more choices than ever, including easy access to legacy and out-of-print material. As creative professionals we have the ability to produce and distribute music without corporate interference, on great-sounding and affordable gear. What's not to like? Besides, we have no choice. The "everyone can be/do everything" model is here to stay. Especially as digital natives (Internet-born citizens of the world) replace the analog aboriginals. Ani DeFranco had it right all along: produce, promote and sell music yourself. Resistance is futile. Long Live the Tail!

Music Radio, RIP

by ROB REINHART

My brother-in-law is a hand surgeon. If you have some injury to your hand or wrist, he's your man. He spends every day, in fifteen-minute intervals, evaluating the human wreckage of twentieth-century manufacturing, with the same repetitive motion injuries being presented to him repetitively. What if, suddenly, a small box allowed a patient to insert his hand into it, and the inner workings of the box made the problems go away? That miraculous box would be everywhere, in the mall, on street corners, at bus stations, and, most important, at the manufacturing facilities that are the source of the problems.

Despite his training and expertise, my brother-in-law would effectively be out of business. Former patients and potential future patients would wave their healthy hands at him. He would receive their greetings half-heartedly, knowing that that small bit of technology changed his life forever. This is how I feel as a veteran of music radio broadcasting. Technology changed everything in an unimaginably short period of time, decimated my industry, and allowed everyone with a computer to become broadcasters and micro-tastemakers. Despite our training and dedication, my peers and I are now, effectively, out of business.

After decades, a perfect storm occurred. It was demographic, technological, economic, and it washed away music broadcasting. As of this writing, it has yet to be replaced by any sort of viable model for financial success. Millions of music websites exist, but I defy you to point to five that are truly economically sustainable. For the sake of argument, let's define *sustainable* as a business that isn't burning through venture capital, or is someone's after-work hobby, but a business creating enough revenue to pay a staff, serve an actual, not virtual, community and create a plan for the future. Like, say, a radio station used to do.

For the last fifteen years I've been the producer and host of a syndicated radio program called *Acoustic Café*. It started as a pursuit of passion, developed as a local program on one station, and blossomed into a syndicated weekly show that has a far-flung network of domestic and foreign affiliates. The show features contemporary and legendary singers and songwriters, displaying their formidable talents for our weekly listeners. *Acoustic Café* is available in new media forms, but it's best heard the way it was intended, over the air. For the record, I never had any venture capital, but would have gladly burned through it if I had. So, undercapitalized but still standing, I'd like to share some thoughts about what happened to my industry and why.

The *Way* the Music Died

I was not one of those hip, underground FM DJ types. Although I respect the spirit and atmosphere that created the underground broadcasting of the late '60s and early '70s, I was too young to be a part of it. I came into this career when a "popular act" toured arena venues and there was a line of those acts a mile long. People queued up for tickets days ahead of time, creating a music/camping experience not unlike what today's twenty-something might experience at Bonnaroo or Wakarusa. But those communal ticketing experiences were free and impromptu, not just part of the process of gaining entry to more than an event, but an exclusive fan club, a community of grassroots supporters of an artist or band. Today, joining a "community" costs folks $350 for the event ticket, with the music simply thrown in as a "value added."

The public anxiously awaited the actual music releases, too. A midnight sale of a new record was another communal experience to be savored. Popular records often sold twenty million or more copies. By comparison, of the 2009 Grammy nominees for Best Album, only two of the five have sold a million copies as of this writing. In short, I came to broadcasting when it was easy to play popular music, and it was a gratifying thing to do so because the public was largely in agreement as to what was popular. In most places in the

United States, music radio died around 2003. Depending on where you stand on the musical snob spectrum, you may place music radio's demise in the 1960s with the rise of Top 40 AM radio. Or "free-form" FM's end in the mid-'70s, which brought us a constant diet of Beatles–Who–Stones–Zeppelin, and later Boston–Foreigner–REO Speedwagon. Some tie music radio's final act to the ascension of MTV and the public's desire to no longer conjure their own images for their music, but instead have it spoon-fed to them by the then fledgling cable outlet. Yet all of those are simply markers in time as radio tried to stay with the changing tastes of the public. It's what all media does to survive and thrive.

Music radio's death came by its own hand in a three-step process. The 1996 Telecommunications Act set the stage, digital technology provided the murder weapon, and short-sighted public companies did the deed. It had little to do with the music itself, just in case you thought I was going to blame the whole mess on Journey, Matchbox 20, or the Jonas Brothers.

The Telecommunications Act of 1996

The Telecommunications Act of 1996 provided the opportunity for a select group of private companies to become public companies and use shareholder money to build broadcasting empires, creating corporately owned chains of stations from hundreds of what were once locally owned stations. It was a textbook example of a greed-fueled buying spree, aided by the creation and passage of this congressional act. For many, the administration of George W. Bush represented the worst kind of laissez-faire atmosphere. But for broadcasters, the Clinton administration ushered in the end of our industry. The act, which had more to do with cable, Internet, and telephone communications, also eliminated most of the ownership rules that had, for more than sixty years, ensured that no one company or individual would hold undue influence over any given broadcast market. In the years following the passage of the Telecomm Act, the United States saw an increase in the number of commercial radio stations (to nearly eleven thousand), but the number of owners for those stations actually decreased by 35 percent.

In the late '90s, it was not uncommon to read articles in radio-industry trade magazines filled with station staffers complaining about the downsizing that was happening within their market. In the age of consolidation, one program director was put in charge of three stations or more, only one of which was playing music he or she actually knew. Music was an afterthought for these overworked program directors, and because most of the choices were being done by a corporate music director a thousand miles away, why even bother having the afterthought? It would just add more unpaid chores to their week. This scenario was taking place in the good times immediately following passage of the Telecomm Act. As the Internet and iPod revolution began to take hold, the do-more-with-less downsizing would accelerate exponentially.

I recall one particularly insensitive, newly minted CEO at one of these Telecomm Act–created broadcasting behemoths dismissing an employee's futile desire for a reversal of the act by saying simply, "It's an act of Congress; deal with it." While the employee was legitimately concerned about now doing three jobs rather than one, the CEO was being applauded by his shareholders. It's good to be king.

I actually got out of my day-to-day radio station job before all of this deregulation and consolidation started. In the early '90s, I had noted a problem with the formation of what we called duopolies and triopolies. These could be likened to consolidation, but done locally between two or more local owners. It was an attempt to trim expenses, with stations often sharing sales, air, and engineering staffs. At the time I found these arrangements to be fundamentally anti-competitive, as you were then expected to join forces with your former cross-town rival, but I admired local broadcasters working together to support their industry in their own market. Unfortunately, this primitive form of consolidation helped acclimate radio folks to the idea of stations' "clustering" together and the corporate version of consolidation to come. This latter, less homespun version saw the benefits of shared sacrifice going only to investors and top managers of companies headquartered in far away locales.

Digital Technology and the Loss of the DJ

The first digital production system I experienced was at an audio dealer, where my business partners and I were assembling the gear for our first studio. We were buying thirty to forty thousand dollars of analog equipment: tape machines, mixing boards, microphones, and the like. In the mid-'80s, if you wanted to assemble a tiny recording studio, that was the minimum you could expect to invest. Now, of course, I'm writing these words as I'm mixing this week's *Acoustic Café* program and balancing my company's books simultaneously on the same bit of equipment, an Apple MacBook Pro. Twenty-five years later, the tape machines are in storage and the mixing board I finally gave to a young guy who thought it might be fun to restore, as one might try to coax the lights and crystals to life in a 1930s Philco cathedral radio.

But at the audio dealership that day in 1986, the staff thought that people spending forty thousand dollars would surely like to see what a hundred thousand might buy them, since after all, it was the future. The digital editor sat in a conference room. It was a mixing desk with computer screens and analog VU (volume unit) meters, probably ten feet long. It was intimidating but fascinating in the same way as the controls you see on a tourist's visit to NASA are. Just when I began to get my mind around this thing, they noted that this was just the "head unit." The actual brains and power

for making ones and zeros into useable audio was housed
outside the room. The staff then introduced me to a rack of
computer gear just slightly smaller than a Mini Cooper. It
hummed, clicked, and whirred so loudly that it required a
separate room in which to operate, so as not to disturb the
talent that might be making that useable audio in the first
place. Come to think of it, an idling Mini Cooper is quieter.
So to total it up: $100K for the gear, added rent for storage,
and it might be handy to have a $50K/year engineer on
hand in case anything went awry. The future was going to be
expensive, or so it seemed at the time.

These amazing tools quickly came down in price. By the
time our little audio production business bought our first
digital editing system nine years later, it was a tenth of the
cost, and could be powered by a normal-size office computer.
It revolutionized the art of audio production, quickly replacing
all of the technology that had preceded it since the 1940s.
There are other writers presented here who can debate the
quality issues of a digital versus analog recording. But from the
perspective of a broadcast producer, there is no question about
the dimension of speed and efficiency that was introduced by
these devices.

Unfortunately, the efficiency wasn't kept in the production
rooms of radio stations. It spread quickly to the larger operation. Digital broadcast systems allowed entire music libraries
to be loaded onto a single hard drive. The switch of a musical
format only required swapping some hardware. Albums and
CDs were no longer necessary, as only the relevant single

songs for a given format needed to be included on that drive. Eventually, this wouldn't even need to be done on site, allowing stations to play material from the central corporate dispenser of sanctioned music.

By the late '90s the on-air digital broadcasting systems also contained the other elements commonly heard in a radio broadcast besides music. Commercials, promotional announcements, "stingers," and most important, the on-air hosts themselves, all became part of the modern computerized radio station. There was a time in the late '70s and early '80s when all but the most addled knew when they were listening to an automated radio station. This primitive, analog automation could only play one element at a time, so these stations creaked along at a snail's pace. Not coincidentally, these stations often played what we would all know as "elevator music," so "snail's pace" fit the station profile perfectly.

By contrast, the automation of today is fast moving and seamless. Even to the trained ear, there is no clue that your local station is, literally, on autopilot. The cluster of stations in my town generally have no humans on site from seven p.m. until five the next morning, and almost no one present all weekend. The air staff now use these digital tools to do what is commonly called voice tracking. Voice tracking is basically recording what they would normally say after a song or before a commercial, without having to wait the real time between their parts. An on-air personality can record a whole four-hour shift in roughly twenty minutes, which allows them the opportunity to do other chores around the station.

So why is this a problem? Voice trackers no longer need to know anything about the music they are playing. All they need is the song title and artist. They don't choose the music, so creating a clever, compelling or a musically logical combination of tunes is no longer an option. Because there is no need to sit through the music, DJs never really get to hear it, so they often don't know a whit about the songs they're playing (unless they choose to learn, on their own time and dime, by the way). In short, through technology, radio has become something that can be done by anyone, anywhere, no knowledge needed... which sounds, ironically, like the worst of web radio!

It used to be that the intimate knowledge of music, radio formats, and simply communicating was learned on overnight or weekend shifts at a radio station. It was where you learned the craft. Replacing these crucial graveyard shifts with voice-tracked, digitally delivered efficiency has confronted the radio industry with another unpleasant reality: There is no next generation of broadcasters. That voice-tracked shift, tacked on to the morning host's exhausting week, has replaced the training ground for the passion-filled broadcaster-to-be. It's worth noting that having these young talents in any operation helps invigorate the entire enterprise. New talent used to come to their radio job with an enthusiasm for music and a need to communicate that enthusiasm. There's a reason they are called "new blood."

The Public Company's Need to Feed

As I write this, almost every publicly traded, pure-play radio broadcasting company is in danger of being delisted from its respective stock exchanges. Most are, literally, trading for pennies. Even this decade's two celebrated satellite radio companies have become one, Sirius/XM. Having barely escaped bankruptcy, their combined financial might works out to about fifteen cents per share. The market has spoken.

Once the Telecomm Act–fueled buying spree was completed around 2003 and the staffing cuts provided shareholders savings through the use of digital technology, the mammoth broadcasters began to load up their stations with commercials. In some cases, eighteen to twenty-two minutes of each hour might be devoted to commercial announcements, despite constant audience rejection of these frequent interruptions. The logic was that, outside of the satellite services that charged consumers for commercial-free music channels, what was a listener's other option? For a time, it worked. Stocks soared and the old broadcast model appeared far from extinction.

This story has been played out in many different businesses during the twentieth century. Lobby for corporately beneficial changes at the governmental level, float the needed capital on Wall Street, then execute changes on Main Street that will create the money flow back to the top. But unlike other industries, radio was supposed to be a business operated locally and in the public interest. Remember, the commercial airwaves are owned by the public, and the government licenses those airwaves to broadcasters, with which they can make money. That privilege, in theory granted by the citizenry, comes with a responsibility to the city of license, rather than the place where the corporate office is located. Or that's how it used to be. Local communities still count on their hometown radio stations, but listeners in those communities have yet to realize that they could now equate their local stations with, say, their local Wal-Mart or their local McDonald's. Like those other mega-businesses, corporate radio stations are simply the drop box for local businesses to send their dollars to San Antonio, Atlanta, or wherever.

Even with the power of a congressional mandate and lots of Wall Street capital, these broadcasting companies failed to note the rise of the Internet. At the turn of the twenty-first century, with the public's access to broadband still low and the commercial revenue still rolling in, the radio companies continued to operate in their old business model. A few radio groups and individual stations began to put up websites; but without clear direction about streaming and content rights, companies felt exposed to litigation, so they went through a cautious period of "on again, off again" web experimentation. The caution crippled the companies and slowed their growth into the new medium, while their e-competition, with no knowledge of or care for laws such as the Digital Millennium Copyright Act, continued to stream their "broadcasts" from basements and work cubicles around the world.

How could these wizards of corporate mass-communications have missed the single biggest revolution in human communicative history? I first heard music delivered through a website in December 1994. It was simply a friend showing me this new thing called the Internet. I remarked that this would change everything (and now kick myself for not jumping in then, but alas...). How Clear Channel, CBS, Infinity, and so on, with all of their resources, could have missed this entirely will be forever a mystery. Didn't they bother to read *the rest* of the Telecomm Act of 1996? Maybe they did and they just didn't understand the new terms: *broadband, wireless, mobile.* It's as if they worked out their radio deregulation piece of the legislation, then turned to the Internet folks in the room and said, "Good luck with that thing... maybe we'll see you at the next convention," before scurrying off to build their short-lived empires.

The corporations can't begin investing in human capital now. It's too late. Recently, it's been a popular consultant's mantra: Radio must create more compelling content for the listener to hear. But, sadly, there are no longer enough people in the business to create all of this new, compelling content. A whole generation of potential content producers—sound artists who would be the most comfortable with digital technology—have not even used radio casually, let alone considered it as an outlet for their creativity. So, going forward, it would appear that the only thing digital broadcast tools will create is the continuance of fewer operators operating more stations more efficiently with fewer people.

In early 2009, the radio sector isn't even covered by most stock market analysts. The companies are carrying huge debt loads, listenership and revenue are down and continue to decline, while Internet usage continues to rise. Clear Channel, having just eliminated 10 percent of its workforce, would love to get rid of any station property below the Top 30 markets, but there are no buyers. Additionally, the credit crisis has frozen out even the most civic-minded local broadcaster with no plans for hegemony, who might like to try something uniquely suited to their home market.

Another popular consultant's mantra says, "It's nothing personal, it's just business." But for all of radio's history, save the last ten years, radio was the most personal media business of all. In replacing live, local broadcasters with digital technology, perhaps that mantra is now truer than ever: "Nothing personal . . . just business."

Pod People

"Have you seen one of these?"

It was a woman from Columbia Records who was accompanying an artist to our studio for an *Acoustic Café* taping. It was March 2002, and the device she was waving at me was an Apple iPod. She thought it would "save the record industry" because of the storage capability. To demonstrate, she showed me the entire Beach Boys catalog that was loaded on her iPod. To be funny, I asked why this Columbia Records employee had the complete catalog of one of Capitol Record's most enduring acts in her pocket. She answered that her friend worked for the Boys' publisher and loaded it up for her. For free.

Industry saved.

Figure it this way: If an iPod holds five thousand songs, and each was purchased legally, the average person would spend about five thousand dollars to fill up one iPod. Who has an extra five grand to buy music? So, of course, people fill their iPods with stolen music. I know it's unpopular to call music lovers thieves, but it's simply the truth. This music is created as a product, which a musician or the musician's supporting company is attempting to sell, and by not paying for it, you're stealing it, period. Actually, that way of thinking is "so 2003." At this point, music was generally accepted as a loss leader, a freebie, to entice you to attend a concert, buy a T-shirt, or join a mailing list.

The iPod created this new environment, ending sixty years of selling recorded music. As it destroyed the music business, the device claimed music broadcasting as collateral damage. The Internet had largely disconnected the public from the local experience, Napster trained an entire generation that music was downloadable and free, and the iPod allowed all that music to be kept in the smallest of pockets. Plus the iPod is cool. Per usual, Apple created a beautiful, functional device that became a "must-have" item and remains so today. The device is far more essential to some than the music stored upon it. While we used to blare our identity through music, we now wear our identity as a Nano, Mini, Touch, or Phone.

So, ever a slave to fashion, radio thought it would get involved with the iPod hoopla. In '02, I recall a program director's telling me that the station was "getting in on the ground floor" with iPods. What I didn't have the heart to say was that this was the ground floor of a private building where the station wasn't welcome, and the "up" elevator had left without it, rocketing its listeners to the penthouse. Many stations, desperately eager to jump on the iPod bandwagon, gave the devices away as promotional items! They might as well have said, "Listen to Q-107 for your chance to win an iPod, so you won't have to listen to Q-107 ever again!!!" They used to give away radios.

What Changed and What Didn't

While the introduction of digital technology permanently changed the art of creating and delivering broadcasts, the notion that digital technology changed the art of listening is an illusion. The digital delivery of music has created many new places to hear, but listening is the same as it's been since people began to listen to electronic devices at the start of the last century. Just because you can hear music on the computer, on the radio, via an iPod, in the mall, in the coffee shop, and on the street corner doesn't change the fact that you can only hear one song at a time and stay sane.

For seventy years, the physics of radio remained unchanged, too. We broadcast on this end, you listen on that end. Even the introduction of magnetic tape in the 1940s didn't change the fundamentals. Although Bob Hope and Bing Crosby did their show on a Saturday night and were coming through your speakers on a Tuesday, they did actually *do* the show that you were hearing in real time. They just saved it for a few days. But in the ten years from the mid-'90s through the mid-'00s, digital technology entirely changed the way broadcasters did their job, despite the fact that the audience was still listening the same way. It would be as if that Hope and Crosby show in the '40s was created by having Hope cut his lines on one day, Crosby cut his on another, adding music at a different time, and an announcer still later. Even if you haven't heard one of those old variety shows, you can imagine what a disconnected mess this type of time-shifted production would be.

The audience would still be hearing the same way, but what they'd be hearing wouldn't, couldn't, have the magic and spontaneity of Hope and Crosby live and in real time. This is what has happened to digitized radio broadcasters. They've lost any connection to what it is that they're broadcasting. The audience that remains, however, is still hearing the same way they always did. If they have a pre-1995 frame of reference, all they know is that it just doesn't sound like it used to. And they're correct. The radio audience, any audience, people in general, want real connections. They used to be able to get that through the radio. If you found a music host that played music you liked, you could count on him to be a companion, and augment the music with information about the artists or the weather or the community, in real time. Someone working the overnight shift wants to listen to someone else living the same life, fighting the same fight, so to speak. But thanks to digital voice tracking, the "overnight guy" simply isn't there, and the overnight shift workers who *are* there are listening to someone who's been in bed for hours. The listener is working, and the broadcaster is sleeping. What's wrong with that picture?

Broken Trust

For more than eighty years, radio was a trusted friend and source. Few stop to think that that trust wasn't just a device to hold an audience, but part of the mandate of every radio station licensed in the United States. Station operators were expected to run their station in the public's interest and diligently serve their local population. After all, those airwaves are owned by the public, and the government is only letting those station owners use them.

To this day, laughable as it may seem, each station is still required to keep a public file on the premises, available for public inspection, detailing what the station has done to serve their community. When I first started in radio in the early '80s, I was once asked to update our station's public file.

Even though we were a rock station, the owner sat me down and gave me a short lecture about the importance of this record. And as a twenty-one-year-old, I was shocked by what I found in that file.

Although I thought I was working for the station that played more Rush and U2 than any other (!), in fact, the station was also presenting programs that were serving the student and elderly populations in our college town. We did a fair amount of local news coverage and public service announcements, and presented events to benefit local non-profit organizations. I never realized how connected we were to the community, and how much the community counted on that connection. That's not to say that this work isn't being done by stations today, but now, with station ownership likely to be absentee and local staffs reduced to skeletal levels, the mandate to work in the public's interest has become much harder to execute. The trust has been broken.

People don't really trust big national banks. Or car companies. Or brokerage firms, politicians, network news anchors, and the large chain store where they now have to buy everything. They expect certain things from these people and institutions, but they don't trust them and aren't surprised when their tenuous trust is broken. Radio used to be a different animal. Local radio was once run by your friends, neighbors, and fellow community participants. They were there every day, talking *to* you and hoping to hear *from* you, in real time. Even the local newspaper, perhaps the most trusted source in most twentieth-century towns, didn't offer a real-time exchange of thoughts, ideas, and culture. If gaining someone's trust is best done face to face, voice to ear is a close second.

It was the new digital technology that permitted this trust to be broken. Like the iPod, the mere introduction of digital broadcast technology would eventually force the changes with which we're now living. I'm not one to blame technology, as it's just as good or useful as the intentions of the person using it. And that's where the blame ultimately lies. The folks who were charged with deploying this new stuff did so with a different mandate than that of public service. They used the technology to trim expenses, consolidate operations, duplicate programming, and eliminate personnel, eviscerating the notion of serving a community.

As for music, the eighteen- to thirty-four-year-olds don't trust radio to play relevant new music. They don't even use radio, let alone trust it to deliver information on music, news, or anything else. It's not that they trust the Internet sources, either, necessarily, but they do trust their friends, and their friends are all on the web. Radio was once a trusted friend. The man or woman behind that microphone helped the listener to select, prioritize, and contextualize the massive amounts of music available in your typical record store. Now, with tens of millions of musicians offering their wares for free through MySpace and the like, and no effective or trusted filters available, the audience has splintered into millions of micro-niches. Some call this the democratization of information. Others call it a Tower of Babel. To-*may*-to, to-*mah*-to.

Rebuilding Trust

So how can the radio broadcasters rebuild the trust of their community? The answer to that has yet to be discovered due to the fact that most broadcasters are just now recognizing that no one trusts them. But for those who are looking ahead, the key is to return to the local nature of the medium. In so doing, they may have to put some of this digital technology aside, or use it in a very different way.

Future-focused broadcasters must involve the youngest members of their communities. I think that local radio stations should use every opportunity to perform public service and outreach. They should be connected and committed to community nonprofits. They should be in the schools, enlisting the help of high school and college students, and providing them as many opportunities to sit behind a microphone as they can. Radio needs the spark and enthusiasm of young broadcasters' experiencing the joy of actually talking to people in real time about ideas that mean something to them. These students are full of great ideas, and will use their active social networks to tell everybody what they're doing and when, which will bring new people to the station as listeners. It's not a podcast, which anyone can do, it's R-A-D-I-O, which is special because it still is the singular, most efficient way to talk to a locale. It stands aside from the Tower of Babel that has been built up around it. This is not wistful harkening to the past, but eagerly anticipating the bright voices and ideas to be heard in the future.

A Positive Ending

If you've read this far, I am grateful. And to express my gratitude, I'd like to end on a positive note about the art of broadcasting in the twenty-first-century.

Lately, I've become fascinated by the concept of what I call drive-by communication. I wish I'd coined that phrase, but I see it mentioned on a couple hundred websites at this point, so I'll consider myself in the vanguard, if not an originator. It's a simple concept to grasp. Facebook, text messaging, e-mail, Twitter, and so on, are designed to communicate in the way one would if driving by a friend on the street at 20 miles per hour. "Hey... How are you? Great... Are you going to the party tonight? See you then. Bye!" It's what digital communication does best. But what we already know is that people really want connection, the ability to hear and exchange longer thoughts and ideas. Public radio does this incredibly well, and it's no small thing that its audience has been growing over the years of this century's first decade. If radio is dead, how could this be so?

Radio's key to survival will be its unique ability to be local. Groups that operate large-scale, satellite-delivered programming will lose, and eventually lose their signal to local broadcasters. Internet radio is already passé. With radio listening applications available for the iPhone now, why would people want to listen to a Clear Channel station from Pittsburgh that sounds just like the one in, say, Houston, when they could listen to WYEP or WDUQ, public stations done live, just for Pittsburgh? It won't matter so much what device delivers the broadcast, but how unique and local that broadcast is. This may require all of the largest group owners to fail, which appears to be happening anyway. After that, the committed, local broadcaster, should be able to pick up a station for a price that doesn't require public money and huge debt. In the '90s, a few thought they'd make a killing consolidating the radio industry. Maybe in the '10s, many will simply make a living in this revitalized medium.

And finally, it should be noted that humans don't evolve nearly as fast as does the technology they develop. We are the same as we've been for fifty thousand years. Just because we now have these nifty devices doesn't mean that we have changed physiologically, emotionally, or sociologically. We can still only hear one song at a time, we understand the spoken word better than the e-mailed sentence fragment, and we crave human connections that are real, not virtual. If digital devices change these fundamentals, we've got bigger problems on our hands than the demise of radio broadcasting. I'd prefer to go forward, believing that future digital technology will enhance human connections rather than add more distance, and that the voices helping to connect us will be in the air, for free, to be heard by all.

Here's hoping.

An End—
a Beginning

by WILLIAM ACKERMAN

Sunlight

I remember seeing the original *Hunchback of Notre Dame* with Charles Laughton. There's a scene in which those about to be beheaded are taken in a horse-drawn wooden cart into a square, the architecture of which is dominated by the guillotine. The aesthetic of the film is very pre-Freddy so that it relies on black-and-white images to make its point. A man is led from the cart up a flight of wooden stairs. His feet land unsurely as he approaches the guillotine.

He kneels and his head is placed in the rounded bottom of the stock. The camera climbs up the guillotine to the gleaming blade. The camera is still as the blade falls and we hear only the sound of sharpened steel reaching the bottom, severing the head from the body and landing on a block of hardwood. The camera is now 20 feet away and we see the head fall into a wicker basket. Even as a child I was perverse enough to wonder for a short while whether there was enough oxygen and blood in the brain and the ocular nerve so that the last thing the head saw was not the planking at his feet as he knelt, but the sun pouring dappled light through the wicker basket.

This is the very moment I believe we find the record business in.

Big Tires

The record business as we know it (or knew it) was really born in the 1960s. Until that time, LPs were more or less throwaways. The business was all about the selling of singles in the form of 45 rpm records that decorate walls of diners these days. People bought LPs, to be sure, but in very limited numbers. They bought the LPs in the vain hope that a single they heard on the radio might have a listenable companion or two on the LP. Such was rarely the case. Then four long-haired guys from Liverpool brought out an LP on Capitol Records in 1964 and everything changed, because every song on that record was wonderful and nearly every one of those songs was played on the radio. Suddenly the notion of an LP's being a suite of music was born, and the old model of one good song cynically packaged among throwaways as a bit of financial gravy for the labels was put to pasture.

The labels all enjoyed incredible growth and artistic prosperity over decades and then, inevitably, in a business dominated by men, testosterone took over. Comparisons to Italian tower building in the Renaissance and big tires on jacked-up rigs are apt. Someone high up in a glass building decided one day that "market share" was the name of the game and a feeding frenzy began in the 1980s, wherein the major labels gobbled up nearly every independent record label to boost this hallowed market share. They continued in this way until they ran out of indie labels to buy and then turned hungrily upon one another. The net result was that there are now less record labels in the world than are represented by the fingers on one hand. Everything is centralized and homogenized (don't get me started on Clear Channel and SoundScan). The record buyers saw the source of their music, justifiably, as a megalith.

The major labels, having inherited the mountain of records once generated by all the indie labels they acquired, and by the merging of one another, were overwhelmed with "product" to pump into their pipelines. To simply dump a record into the marketplace without support of marketing and promotion is arguably financial suicide, but increasingly this is what took place, with an inordinate number of records' being condemned to nearly certain oblivion. Priorities had to be established: what was selling in the moment was the priority, and holding onto that thread was the key to survival.

186 Less Noise, More Soul

The musical landscape shrank. Those little indie labels, once purchased for their contribution to a wide-spectrum musical market, were relegated to secondary and tertiary roles and then forgotten. Certainly Def Jam and other indies had a great deal to do with the emergence of hip-hop and rap, but what is left is only the tip of a pyramid that once effectively marketed a wide range of musical styles.

The challenges of the Internet and downloading brought overwhelming change and only drove the major labels further into a conservative posture.

That artists including the Eagles (and Will Ackerman) have jumped ship and made deals with Target and Walmart stores, that James Taylor released a CD sold exclusively via Hallmark, and that Sir Paul McCartney announced that his music will be sold by Starbucks pretty much tells the story. It's over.

Out of the Ashes

Here's my dream. I think it's really quite possible.

Like everything else in publishing these days, the Internet will break apart what is left of the megalith's narrow focus. Specialized websites will (and are) emerging to cater to and promote a vast array of musical interests and will generate an artistic renaissance. New indie labels will proliferate via the Internet and the musical landscape will become richer again.

Kids brought up in a time of conservative and narrow focus will embrace a new ecumenicalism.

These same kids will understandably cease to see the source of their musical loves as part of a megalith. They will be communicating with the artists directly via websites, weighing in on which songs they like best and picking their favorite from among a selection of mixes of different songs. The artists themselves will be creating their own record labels and will again be seen by their fans as flesh-and-blood human beings with families to support. Downloading of singles will continue but, increasingly, methods of rewarding the artists and acknowledging their copyrights will be respected. Then one day, some young musician will get a brilliant new idea: "What if I took twelve songs and put them together in a single package and created a long-form musical experience..."

Coda:
Gangland Hit

by CLIFFORD F. ADAMS

There's a way out of this," he muttered to himself. "I know there is."

J. T. Bigge and his staff sat around the huge Brazilian walnut conference table. The only sounds were the squeaks and creaks of the buttery leather chairs each time one of them fidgeted. A cloud of smoke hung above their heads. Comfortably ensconced at the head of the table, Bigge wore a handmade tropical suit. He stuck a smoldering Cuban cigar in the corner of his mouth. He fiddled with his yellow silk tie and absently adjusted his gold tie clasp. He puffed the big cigar, plucked it from his mouth with tobacco-stained fingers, and exhaled a curled plume of white smoke that, for a fleeting instant, resembled a swan.

He owned the *Rosie O'Donnell Show*—for better or for worse.

His staff simply called him Bigge. He spat a tiny bit of tobacco from the tip of his tongue. All eyes cast anxious glances at him and then refocused on the face of his assistant, who was perched next to him looking miserable.

Her cell phone shattered the silence. *Back that ass up!*, its ring tone chanted. *Back that ass up!... Back that ass up!...*

"Aw, for the love of God, answer it, will you?" Bigge snapped, his voice rising.

"Hello," she squawked. "What did she say?"

Fidget. "Omigod."

Squirm. "And you told her that it wasn't in her contract?"

Gasp. "Rosie actually said that? She didn't give a..." She rolled her eyes, avoiding the stare of her boss. "He's not going to be happy about this." She disconnected and gingerly placed the cell phone on the table in front of her.

"Damn," Bigge muttered, shaking his head.

"Sorry," croaked the assistant, ducking her head.

Bigge touched a button—"Send Watson in here," he ordered. "The rest of you can..."

John Watson joined the staff of the *Rosie O'Donnell Show* right out of tech school. He, like many audio engineers, was fully 7 feet tall. He was athletic, sandy-haired, blue-eyed, and strikingly handsome. The basketball coach at his former high school, unable to persuade him to join the team, gave in to despair and hanged himself.

Watson took to audio production quite naturally because of the extraordinary length of his arms, which spanned all of 7 feet, 2¾ inches. No button, knob, switch, or fader was beyond his grasp. He didn't need an assistant to do anything except stay out of the way.

Watson descended, lunar lander–like, into a chair. "You wanted to see me, Bigge?"

"Rosie wants to sing."

"Aw, nuts," Watson groaned. He collapsed dramatically onto the conference table and buried his face in his forearms.

"Yeah, the broad's terrible. Thing is, she knows it." Bigge puffed his cigar, then turned it around for visual confirmation that it was evenly lit. "And she knows she's got us. So, we gotta make a silk purse out of a sow's ear, Watson," Bigge said with a shrug. "What can we do?"

"Bigge, she just *sucks*," Watson whined.

"On that we agree, son," he chuckled. "So, what can we do?"

"I don't know." Watson sighed heavily. "Unless . . ."

"Unless what? Have you got something?"

Yes, I have something, Watson thought. He steepled his long fingers in front of his chest and said simply, "I can pitch-shift her."

"What's that?" muttered Bigge.

"I'll pitch-shift her." His face brightened and a smile flirted with the corners of his mouth.

"And that will . . ." Bigge prompted.

"It will correct all her out-of-tune notes," replied Watson.

"You mean—she'll be more in tune?"

"I mean, she'll be perfectly in tune," affirmed Watson.

"Anyone done this kind of thing before?"

"Yeah. Cher."

"Cher? When? *Cher?* Hell, I thought Cher was *dead*."

"No, no, Bigge, she's still around. She had her lips done, is all."

"Oh . . . *that's* who that is . . ." Bigge's voice trailed off.

It was three o'clock the next afternoon when his receptionist buzzed: "Bigge, John Watson to see you."

"Good. Send him in."

Watson ducked through the doorway into Bigge's private office. "I got video."

"And?" prompted Bigge from his chair behind his huge desk.

"It's going to be fine, but see for yourself," he nodded confidently.

In one space-defying motion, Watson stretched his left arm past Bigge and slipped a DVD into a player, while his right arm positioned the monitor so they both could see. He pressed the Play button as he folded his lanky frame into a chair.

For the next three minutes, the two men watched intently. The star stood next to a grand piano on an empty soundstage. The intro to the old standard, "Fever," tinkled from the speakers and the star of the *Rosie O'Donnell Show* began to sing.

Bigge was stunned. It was thrilling to hear. The performance sounded like Rosie, but a new, improved Rosie. In tune? Yes. Timing? Perfect. Phrasing? Immaculate.

Bigge stared at the monitor. "How'd you do that?"

"Like I said: I pitch-shifted her. It's a computer process," he began, "that . . ."

"Yeah, yeah, computers," Bigge interrupted. "Who cares how you did it. You did it. Too bad she still looks like Jackie Gleason, 'cause I'll be damned if she doesn't sound like Peggy Lee!"

At exactly the same moment, one floor down from Bigge's top-floor office, Carey Nation burst into the office of Bogart Martin, who was head of A&R★ in the music division, and her boss. She bounced and jiggled across the plush black carpet and busied herself at his private bar.

Men like Bogart Martin were hard to find. Known simply as Bogie to everyone in the industry, it was said that he could single-handedly lift the music business out of a funk and nudge the public into a purchasing frenzy. He had a track record. He had the knack. His formula? Just do it. How? Fake it 'til you make it. And keep your eyes, ears, and above all, your options, open.

Bogie's close-cropped, graying hair bespoke experience and capability. His blue eyes and a ready smile made him instantly likeable. Awards—more than he bothered to count—lined his office walls.

Bogie took in the show as Carey expertly conjured a pitcher of martinis at the bar. He loved Carey's contagious

★Artists & Repertoire

enthusiasm. He also loved her legs. You wouldn't have to press very hard to make him admit that he also admired her breasts.

He'd brought her on board recently, not even bothering to read her résumé. He only wondered about one thing— was she really as ditzy as she seemed, or was it an act? Time will tell, he believed, and she makes a hell of a martini.

"Make one for yourself, too," he prompted.

"Thanks, I did," she giggled, tasting it, and then setting up another glass. "This demo just came FedEx." She leaned over his desk and handed him a small package. "Can we listen?" Carey never missed a chance to listen to the stuff that crossed his desk. He often found that he enjoyed her company more than the music.

"Okay." Bogie swiveled around and inserted the disc into a player. As he spun back around, Carey leaned over his desk again, put the martini in front of him, and shot him a second generous glimpse of sun-freckled cleavage. For a moment, he smelled roses in Calaveras County. His head spun. He took a sip. Yep. Hell of a martini.

They listened casually at first, then attentively. A minute passed and Bogie looked at her, a frown creasing his face. He cocked his head. "Sounds familiar, doesn't it, Carey?"

"It's Ray Charles, isn't it?" she offered.

He nodded. "But I've heard these *tracks* before," he said, touching a finger to his lips.

"It's definitely Ray Charles," she said, bouncing her breasts helpfully.

"Ray Charles," he echoed, thoughtfully. He rubbed his fashionably unshaven salt-and-pepper chin. "Wait a second!" he exclaimed, knocking over his martini. "This is . . ." His mouth opened in surprise. Then, instantly in full-on business mode, "Find out who did this, Carey. Get me the number. Right away! And get a copy of this to Bigge!"

And that, in a nutshell, is how Bogie "discovered" techno wizard Esteban Santa Cruz, though he'd never tell it.

Bogie managed to get in an early round of golf the next morning. After showering and dressing, he called to confirm his appointments. On the road, he threaded his platinum Porsche through schools of slower traffic, his hands drumming the steering wheel to the music on the radio. He went through the gears one last time as he roared down the street, making his approach. He skidded into the lot and screeched to a halt in his private parking space, revving the engine once more before shutting it down.

Bogie strode from his car under a cloudless blue sky. At the door, he turned and looked longingly at the Porsche, and, for just a moment, he thought about getting back in the car and spending the rest of the day driving.

A few minutes later, a receptionist ushered in his first appointment, Esteban Santa Cruz.

"Cruz, thanks for coming by," Bogie greeted him with a smile and a handshake. "Love the new Ray Charles. Sit, sit," Bogie gestured toward a chair.

Esteban Santa Cruz affected an upscale "gaucho amigo" in spangled leather, bolo tie with a turquoise clasp, Tony Lama boots, and aged Wranglers. He smelled like expensive leather. As he eased into a seat, his dark ponytail draped down behind the chair, halfway to the floor. He removed his sunglasses to reveal alert black eyes.

Bogie seated himself and leaned forward, resting clasped hands on the desk in front of him.

"Interesting project, Cruz, Ray Charles covering Sinatra's *Duets*. But I've never heard any Ray Charles recordings of these songs. Where'd you get them?" asked Bogie.

"Trade secret." Cruz flashed a gleaming smile.

"Ah," breathed Bogie, smiling back.

"It's done with a computer. It's proprietary—mine," said Cruz. "It's the audio equivalent of putting an actor's head on a model's body and then touching it up with Photoshop."

"You mean that is not Ray singing?"

"That's right. That is Sinatra's vocal track, modified by yours truly," said Cruz.

"But that was Ray's voice on 'Come Rain or Come Shine,' wasn't it?"

"No," Cruz replied patiently, "it's all Frank." He smiled.

"And you . . ." Bogie gestured.

"Altered it," Cruz obliged, finishing his sentence. "Ray Charles is now singing those duets, with Frank's partners and the original tracks."

Bogie whistled softly. "What will Ray's people say?" he wondered aloud. "And Sinatra's people?"

"That, as they say, is your problem," replied Cruz, his black eyebrows arched.

In the next few minutes, Bogie learned several interesting things about Cruz's invention. What he found most interesting was the fact that no one else had seen it, yet.

"Carey makes a great martini. Will you join me?" offered Bogie.

"Love one," Cruz agreed.

Bogie pressed a button. "Martinis for everyone!" he sang into the intercom.

Bogie stood up. "I need to see Bigge—if he hasn't already gone to lunch," he explained. He made stay-put gestures as he crossed the room. He didn't want this fish to get away. "Relax a minute, have a martini."

Not missing a beat as Bogie dashed out, Carey glided in and sashayed over to the bar.

Cruz took one look at her and momentarily forgot—well, gosh, everything. He grinned foolishly.

"Martinis for everyone!" Carey announced, and beamed a smile back at him.

Bogie dashed up a flight of stairs and popped into Bigge's office. "Have you listened to it?"

"I've listened to it," answered Bigge. "It's nuts. Question is, will they buy it?" Before Bogie could reply he answered his own question. "Yeah, they'll buy it." He surveyed his cigar. "Who is this guy, anyway, this Santa Cruz fellow? What do you know about him?"

"He's downstairs now. He came to us on his own. Computer genius, is my guess," said Bogie.

"Computers," Bigge grunted. He took a big pull on his cigar and his eyes followed as he delicately floated a fat, fluffy cat-shaped cloud toward the ceiling.

"I think we should move on it," said Bogie.

"Lawyers are going to be twitchy," countered Bigge, watching the smoky shape disperse.

"Of course," agreed Bogie. "That's how they earn their money."

"Then let them earn some money before we do anything." He stood and adjusted his shirt cuffs and coat. "Let's go to lunch. Take Cruz with us."

They went downstairs to Bogie's office and found it empty. Cruz and Carey were gone. No message.

The perfect morning gave way to a dark and cloudy afternoon. It looked like rain, so Bigge put up the top on his prized, restored-to-perfection 1956 Thunderbird. He slid into the driver's seat, and the red leather squeaked quietly as he leaned forward to hit the ignition. Bogie got in on the other side.

The wind bent the palms along the boulevard. Lightning spidered the sky and killed a billion mold spores. The ozone-rich air smelled clean. A few dollops of rain splattered the hood and windshield.

Fifteen minutes later, Bigge sat facing Bogie in his favorite booth at Giacomo's, a swank eatery off Rodeo. Valets parked his 'Bird among the Porsches, Jaguars, and Bentleys outside.

Their waitress was a sultry platinum blonde, obviously an aspiring actress.

"See anything thing you like, boys?" she quipped, handing Bigge a menu.

Bigge ordered steak, rare—without breaking eye contact with her. Bogey selected the vegetarian lasagna.

When the waitress left to put in their orders, Bigge turned back to Bogie. "So, you think we ought to move on this?" he prompted.

Bogie turned the corners of his mouth down and shrugged. "I think they're going to love it."

Bigge grunted. That was usually good enough for him, but this time it didn't feel right. He had to put his cigar out before he walked into the restaurant and he was already irritated by a nagging craving. *What has the world come to,* he mused, silently, *when a man can get arrested for smoking a cigar?*

Bogie eyed his boss patiently. *Here it comes,* he thought.

"Did I ever tell you about the time, when I was a kid in college, I worked in a brewery?"

"No, you didn't," replied Bogie, slowly leaning forward, interested. Bigge never talked about himself.

"In my home town, back in the seventies, there were several local breweries and I got a summer job at one of them. Most of the work was stacking beer cases on a conveyor. Machines filled the bottles and put them in cases. Then we loaded them on trucks. The old hands there called me 'Shakespeare' because I was a college kid."

"Sounds like a boring job," said Bogie.

"It wasn't so bad," replied Bigge. "It was hot as the devil that summer, but they gave us breaks in the taproom. We served ourselves cold, fresh, unpasteurized beer. Oh man, that was good beer!"

"They used to pasteurize beer?" asked Bogie.

"Still do. Extends shelf life. I'll tell you, Bogie, people buy what you sell 'em. They buy old beer, they buy light beer. Hell, they even buy raspberry beer! And they drink it like they like it," Bigge said. "Poor sons of bitches don't know what good beer is."

"You really think so?" prompted Bogie.

"I know so," he scoffed. "Now, take this new computer process of Cruz's. You know what I think? It's pasteurized beer. I mean, yeah, you're right of course—people are gonna love it. But I gotta tell you, pasteurized music. That's what it is."

"Does that mean you want to pass on this?" Bogie asked.

"Do you think you can sell it?" countered Bigge.

Bogie answered, separating the syllables, "Absolutely."

Bigge responded with a shrug of his own and a wry grin.

Their meals arrived and Bigge turned his attention to the would-be starlet. She leaned close enough that he could smell her perfume, see the makeup on her face, neck, and shoulders as she placed a sizzling plate in front of him, her heavy cleavage suspended inches from his eye. *Whoa! She's got Marilyn Monroe down pat*, he thought. The steak was still simmering when he attacked it.

Bigge eyed Bogie's plate. "How's the lasagna?"

As Bogie nodded his reply, Bigge glanced around the room, looking for the source of the piped-in light jazz. *Light jazz*, he thought to himself. *Light jazz, my ass.*

After he polished off his steak, Bigge ached for a cigar. He pulled a Cohiba out of his coat pocket and immediately a nearby waiter coughed politely.

"Don't worry, I'm not going to light it," he called softly, waving off the law-enforcing waiter.

Marilyn Monroe reappeared, balancing two martinis on a tray. "These drinks are compliments of a friend," she breathed.

Bigge managed a grateful smile, but didn't notice that her hand trembled as she placed the drink in front of him. He stared across the table in Bogie's direction, looking at nothing, thinking.

"Come on," Bogie prodded, gently. "Spill it. What's on your mind?" The waitress deposited a drink in front of him, too, which he ignored for the moment. His eyes were fixed on the wheels that he could almost hear turning behind Bigge's eyes.

"Dead guys makin' records." Bigge shook his head and sighed. "When mics and amps first came out, they opened a world of new possibilities for artists. Now, Bing Crosby could croon. Louis Armstrong could sing in a nice, conversational style. 'I'm Dreaming of a White Christmas.' 'West End Blues.' Great stuff. Great then, great now. When a singer no longer had to belt it out so the folks in the top row of the cheap seats could hear, he could sing with a lot more expression."

Bigge fumbled his martini, almost spilled it, sloshing a little on the tablecloth, recovered, and took a sip.

"Using a mic, singers could showcase a new kind of musicianship," he continued. "At least it was new to the public; and they loved it. It was loaded with feeling. Sinatra started as a crooner in the thirties. Whispering Jack Smith made records that were big hits way back in the late twenties. The technology was primitive compared to these computers they have now. The recording *process* was different, too, but it was different because the *objective* was different." He stabbed the air with his unlit cigar and took a deep drink of his martini.

"Bigge," Bogie offered, "Maybe you're putting too fine a point on it. Look what you were able to do for Rosie. We saved ourselves a lot of embarrassment *and* we made our star happy." *No small task*, he thought.

Bigge shook his head. "Back when I was getting started, a whole team of experts got involved in preparing for a session: A&R men, writers, arrangers, producers, and engineers. A lot of thought and work went into it before any tape ever started to roll. They created the perfect environment to capture a dynamic, expressive performance, filled with subtle expression and nuance that only great artists could pull off. Who had time to waste on a singer who *couldn't even sing*?"

The question hung there.

"Are you saying that digital technology is ruining the business?" asked Bogie.

"I'm saying I've been around awhile," Bigge continued, "and I've been in a few recording sessions when *magic happened*;

when we knew we'd captured a great performance. We held our breath until the red light went off, then the whole crew spontaneously burst into applause. But now," Bigge eyed the unlit end of his cigar, "now it's up to a computer operator to spruce up some hack's half-assed track after everyone's gone home. You switch on a computer, go take a crap, come back, and you've got a hit." He shook his head. "I'm just wondering, Bogie, if we've thought this through." He finished off his martini.

A door opened, and the cozy ambience of the room slipped out like a house cat. An asphalt-tainted fog crept in like a burglar, hovered above the floor, silently infiltrated the dining room, nuzzling the polished chair legs.

Bogie shivered. *Coffee,* he thought. He tried to get the waitress's eye, but she averted her gaze and walked away.

"Hey, where's she going?" he muttered to himself. People in the booths on both sides of theirs were suddenly getting up to leave. *Everyone wants to beat the storm,* he supposed, *but it's too late.* The lights flickered.

Bigge raised his hand as if to say something, but coughed instead.

Bogie streaked the condensation on his glass with his thumb. "Let's get Cruz under contract," he said. "Maybe it's nothing—maybe it's big, but I'd hate to see him sign with a competitor. Know what I mean?"

Bogie looked up. Bigge's eyes bulged like a Beverly Hills boob job. His face looked like red leather, and veins popped out on his neck and temples. Foamy, blood-stained spittle ran down his chin onto his silk tie. A horrible rasping sound came from his throat.

"Bigge! Jesus! *Bigge!*" he gasped. *"Somebody call 911! Get a doctor!"* He scooted out of the booth and sprang to his feet as Bigge began to seize violently. Bigge's clenched fingers broke his unlit cigar in half, scattering pieces of it on the tablecloth. His back arched, he exhaled wetly and his body went limp, his eyes fixed on the ceiling.

"Help!" Bogie shouted hoarsely.

A small, stocky man walked quickly toward the booth. He wore a crisp dark suit, a dark shirt with a white tie. His black alligator shoes creaked as he stepped up.

"You didn't drink your martini, Bogie," the man said. "What gives? I send drinks and you don't drink yours."

"A man's dying and you're talking about drinks!" Bogie shouted. The man merely shrugged. Bogie pulled out his cell phone and began to dial 911, his hands trembling too violently to punch in the numbers accurately. Then, the little man seemed to spit in his face, and that was the last thing Bogie knew.

Cruz ate dinner alone in his kitchen with a small TV tuned to the news. A crew broadcast live from Giacomo's, where emergency vehicles glittered in the wet parking lot while a crowd of curious locals gawked from the police perimeter. He reached for the TV remote and turned up the volume.

"Officials are saying little as their investigation begins, but witnesses say that two men were killed in Giacomo's during lunch today!" barked a blond reporter, her voice shrill with urgency, her best frown helping to sell her concern. The camera zoomed in on her face as she continued her pitch.

"Police are questioning employees but divulging nothing at this time. However, several witnesses, who wish to remain anonymous, say this was a *gangland hit.*" She paused, her eyes focused on something outside camera range. "Here comes a senior officer now!"

She stepped into the path of a stern-looking cop. "Is it true that it's a gangland hit, Lieutenant?" She thrust the microphone toward his mouth.

"It appears that one man choked to death or was poisoned," he said.

"Poisoned?" repeated the reporter, suddenly more alert, like a shark scenting blood in the water. God, she prayed the cameraman was getting this. "Do you have any details yet?"

"It's under investigation. That's all I can say," he said as he sucked in his stomach.

"What about the second victim?" she pressed him.

"Well, I don't think it would be premature to say that the second victim was shot in the head at close range. That's all I can tell you now." He pushed past the reporter and the camera.

Off-camera, the news anchorman chimed in, "Have the victims been identified?"

"Not officially," she answered, "but one witness, who wishes to remain anonymous, identified the victims as two well-known TV and record executives. We'll have the names as soon as they are released. Stay tuned for more on this story!"

Cruz sat staring in his kitchen chair, a burrito suspended in midair in one hand, the remote in the other, still aimed at the TV. EMTs rolled two stretchers carrying body bags to waiting ambulances. The rain had stopped. Steam rose from the street. Children crowded into the foreground, splashing gleefully in the overrun storm gutter and waving at the cameras, apparently oblivious to the tragedy that had occurred minutes earlier. The ambulances pulled away.

It couldn't be Bigge and Bogie, he considered. *Could it?* "Gangland style," they'd said. *No, that's too crazy. My imagination is getting the best of me*, he decided.

At their meeting that morning, Bogie had made no effort to conceal his enthusiasm from Cruz. If it hadn't been necessary to run it by Bigge, they would have made a deal then and there, thought Cruz. Bogie told him not to worry; just give Bigge a little time to get used to the idea. He'll come around, Bogie promised.

Later, the six o'clock news led with file video of Bigge and Bogie's accepting awards. John Thomas Bigge poisoned! Bogart Martin shot in the head at close range with a small-caliber handgun! "Gangland style!" the anchorman's voice savored the words.

The camera zoomed in for a head shot of Carey in the first sound bite. "I can't believe it," she cried. "It's just so wrong."

"Who would want to kill Mr. Bigge and Bogie Martin?" asked the reporter.

"I simply can't imagine," Carey said, dabbing her eyes with a tissue.

"Had there been any arguments at work, or anything unusual?"

"Nothing at all," answered Carey. "I was with Bogie just before he left for lunch with Bigge. Everything was fine."

"What were Bogie's last words to you?"

"He said he was hungry, and that he'd be back by two o'clock."

Cruz shuddered as he realized that he might have been at lunch with the two men if Carey hadn't invited him first. *Dios mio.* She had probably saved his life today!

At lunch, Carey had probed with questions about his invention, his plans, and, finally, whether he was ready to make a deal. When he said that he was ready to hear an offer, she excused herself and made a call on her cell phone, leaving Cruz to wonder whether she was only an assistant, because she certainly knew how to talk business.

The story of the double homicide was the talk of Tinsel Town, and a few hours later, the entire world.

Evening found Cruz exhausted, and he fell asleep in his old recliner, dead to the world. But his rest was not dreamless. In his dream, a man wearing elegant black evening clothes stood on a beach, gazing at a spectacular sunset over the magnificent, blue ocean. White hair haloed his head.

Just down the beach, two figures appeared and wafted toward them above the surf, their shapes shifting like smoky apparitions. As they drew nearer, Cruz recognized Bigge and Bogie, their eyes wide and unblinking and their faces throbbing with a ghostly pallor.

The man in black slowly raised his arm toward them, accusingly. Then, with a violent, inward twist of his arm, he turned his thumb down in a gesture of unmistakable finality.

Bigge and Bogie collapsed in the shallow surf where sand fleas and ghost crabs began the hideous work of devouring their faces.

Cruz tried to run to them but found he was paralyzed. The man in black turned slowly toward him. Cruz looked directly into the man's blue eyes, which were as brilliant and dazzling as the sea. Holding Cruz's gaze, the man slowly raised his arm.

Cruz jerked upright with a loud gasp, every muscle taut, his heart pounding. The rapid-fire report of heels crossing the porch to his front door beckoned him toward consciousness.

Three raps on the door. Adrenaline still coursed through his veins. Five more raps, louder than before.

"Cruz? It's Carey. Did you watch the news?" She rapped five more times. "Cruz, are you there?"

He turned on the lamp next to the recliner, walked to the door, and peered out through the curtains. A black limo sat at the curb, its parking lights on. He unlocked the door.

"Cruz!" Carey cried. "Have you heard? Bigge and Bogie are . . ." but she couldn't finish.

"Yes," he said, "I saw it on TV. Please, come in."

She threw herself at his chest, slipping her arms around him and holding him tightly. "Hey, easy now," he soothed, "it's going to be all right."

"You feel good," she said.

You feel good, too, he thought, but he didn't say so.

In a few minutes, they agreed that only one thing could settle their nerves—drinks. Later, after several nerve-settling drinks and silent negotiations that involved heavy breathing, they tacitly agreed that sex would do them both a world of good.

AES★ arbiters of good taste in industry-related publications, while exerting no influence of any weight in the direction of censorship, would, nevertheless, prefer to keep distractions to a minimum. Therefore, rather than present an inventory of a heaving this, a trembling that, and a throbbing of the other as the surf crashed in, let it be sufficient to say, then, that Take One was a keeper. Take Two, more controlled and attentive to detail. Take Three, in a mighty stroke, jacked one right out of the ballpark. And Take Four, while not entirely necessary and perhaps a mild exaggeration—albeit one that no one could check—would do as a "safety mix" of sorts.

"There's a lot of potential in your magic," Carey cooed, when they had returned to a more intellectual intercourse.

"You think so?" asked Cruz languidly.

"Oh, yes." She sat up on the couch and patted the space next to her.

He moved over and put his arm around her shoulders.

"There's a group of businessmen in Branson, Missouri," she began, "who want to market your invention in the consumer electronics area."

★Audio Engineering Society

"Consumer electronics? For home use? But it's an audio engineer's tool," he protested.

"Hear me out," she insisted, stroking his leg. "These people are willing to pay you, and pay you well, for exclusive licensing rights to your technology. And no, they are not in the recording industry."

"Well, if they're not in music, then what do they want to do with my technology?"

Carey spent the next thirty minutes describing, in detail, exactly what they planned to do. Cruz was openly appalled at first, but warmed to the idea when she began projecting sales and talking numbers.

They went into the kitchen where Cruz made fresh coffee and two BLTs.

Just after midnight there was a quiet knock at the front door. Carey let out a little yelp of dismay as she bounded barefoot across the floor to answer it. She opened the door to a stocky little man dressed in a dark suit, black shirt and white tie. He wore black alligator shoes. He held his cap in his hand.

"Carlo!" she cried. "I'm so sorry. Have you been waiting all this time?" She turned to Cruz and explained, "Carlo is my driver. I forgot about him, poor thing!"

Carlo grinned sheepishly. "It's okay," he shrugged. "Hey, business is business," he intoned.

Sales of Sound-Like-Elvis karaoke machines passed eighteen million units in the first eight months. No matter who the user was, when he sang into the plastic golden microphone, what emerged from the rhinestone-studded speakers was unmistakably the voice of the King.

Sales knew no demographic boundaries, crossing over age, race, and gender like no other entertainment product in recent memory. The money men in Branson were thrilled and getting richer by the day.

Branson's professional Elvis impersonators tried to unionize. They complained that their audiences had become extremely critical. Box office receipts sagged.

An elderly woman discovered a likeness of Elvis on a grilled cheese sandwich at IHOP. Her story drove sales to new levels and inspired dozens of Sound-Like-a-Star Karaoke Bars. Tourists from all over the world made the pilgrimage to Branson to be transformed into idols before devout audiences of appreciative friends, patient associates, and innocent bystanders.

Cruz sat on the balcony of their Miami penthouse and gazed lazily at several ships lined up waiting for tugboats. A light morning breeze carried up the salty aroma of the ocean and beach below. There wasn't a cloud in sight.

Carey emerged from the apartment carrying a single martini which she handed to him.

"You read my mind, baby," laughed Cruz.

"You're welcome," smiled Carey. "Do you want to do something tonight?"

"I got Broadway tickets," he teased, in a sing-song voice.

"Not for tonight!" she exclaimed in surprise. She let a smile spread across her tanned face.

"For tomorrow. Think you two will feel like it?" he asked, gently placing his hand on her swollen belly.

"Sure!" she squeaked.

"Carlo is getting the plane ready," he said, as he mindfully pulled her down onto his lap and kissed her.

Notes

Introduction

xi "I'll give you more power": *Charlie Rose*, PBS, January 29, 2003.

xii "everybody is equally confused": "Death of the Record Business? Birth of the Music Business," symposium of the Nashville Chapter of the Recording Academy, June 7, 2005, DVD.

xiv "revolution in the head": Ian MacDonald, *Revolution in the Head: The Beatles' Records and the Sixties,* 2nd Rev. Ed. (London: Pimlico, 2005).

xiv "Two things": Rick Bass, *Brown Dog of the Yaak: Essays on Art and Activism* (Minneapolis, Minn.: Milkweed Editions, 1999), 118.

xiv "basic human need": Charles Rosen, *Piano Notes: The World of the Pianist* (New York: The Free Press, 2002), 235.

Less Noise, More Soul

36 "colonized by technology": Ian MacDonald, *Revolution in the Head: The Beatles' Records and the Sixties*, 2nd Rev. Ed. (London: Pimlico, 2005), 34.

36 "The Beatles' way of doing things": *Ibid.*, p. xiii.

37 "The recordings are pretty crappy": Stephen St. Croix, "Quality Software at 10 Percent of Retail Prices," *Mix*, May, 2005, 20.

39 "If one has nothing": Ian MacDonald, interview by Beppi Colli, August 5, 2003, http://www.cloudsandclocks.net/interviews/IMacDonald_interview.html.

40 "organic growth": Howard Bilerman, "Overrated? The Mainstream," EQ, June 2005, 8.

41 "a lot of technique and no soul": Quoted in James Gavin, *Deep in a Dream: The Long Night of Chet Baker* (New York: Alfred A. Knopf, 2002), 352.

41 "does it *mean* anything?": Ian MacDonald, *The People's Music* (London: Pimlico, 2003), 178.

41 "the intensity of experience": Charles Rosen, *Critical Entertainments: Music Old and New* (Cambridge, Mass.: Harvard University Press, 2000), 317.

42 "If you were not so desperate": Quoted in Wolfgang Leppmann, *Rilke: A Life* (New York: Fromm International, 1984), 262.

42 "one needs to have a great life": Daniel Barenboim, *Everything is Connected: The Power of Music* (London: Weidenfeld and Nicolson, 2008), 187.

43 "My proper sense": Jim Harrison, *Off to the Side: A Memoir* (New York: Grove Press, 2002), 228.

44 That these phenomena: See the discussion in MacDonald, *The People's Music*, 207–8.

44 "when the audience changes": Aaron Copland, *Music and Imagination* (Cambridge, Mass.: Harvard University Press, 1952), 107.

44 "Memorable recordings start": Bruce Swedien, *Make Mine Music* (Norway: MIA Musikk, 2003), 14.

44 "The best gear increases": St. Croix, "Quality Software," 20.

44 "All forms of culture": Charles Rosen, *The Frontiers of Meaning: Three Informal Lectures on Music* (New York: Hill and Wang, 1994), 76.

44 "baptism by fire": Bob Spitz, *The Beatles: The Biography* (New York: Back Bay Books, 2005), ch. 12.

45 "I am not sure how much": George Martin and William Pearson, *With a Little Help from My Friends: The Making of Sgt. Pepper* (Boston: Little, Brown, 1994), 13.

46 "constantly in search for perfection": Geoff Emerick and Howard Massey, *Here, There and Everywhere: My Life Recording the Music of The Beatles* (New York: Gotham Books, 2006), 369.

46 "The records that sold": Reported by bandmate David T. Dominy.

46 Indeed, George Martin feels: Emerick, *Here, There and Everywhere*, 191. An even earlier display of exemplary ingenuity may be found, across the Atlantic, in the seemingly self-evident production of the Del Shannon icon, "Runaway"; see Brian Young, "Classic Tracks: Del Shannon, 'Runaway,'" *Mix*, October 2008, 76–79.

49 "To me, to be important": Swedien, *Make Mine Music*, 206.

50 "The old musical instrument makers": Ibid., 150.

52 "In fact, the more processing you do": Quoted in Kevin Becka, "Guitar Greatness," *Mix*, March, 2005, 34.

52 "the Fifth Voice": John Phillips, *Papa John* (Garden City, N.Y.: Dolphin Books, 1986), 137.

52 "Technology was made for man": Thomas Merton, *Conjectures of a Guilty Bystander* (New York: Image Books, 1989), 222.

53 "Wicked Game": Maureen Droney, "Classic Tracks: Chris Isaak's 'Wicked Game,'" May 1, 2002, http://mixonline.com/recording/interviews/audio_chris_isaaks_wicked/

53 "If it *sounds* right": Gavin, *Deep in a Dream*, 35.

53 "The difference between Sixties pop": MacDonald, *Revolution in the Head*, 388.

53 "Your music was like": *Paul McCartney in Red Square*, DVD (A&E, 2005).

53 "I do get emotional": The Beatles, *Anthology* (San Francisco: Chronicle Books, 2000), 356.

54 "We must dare to think": J. William Fulbright, *Old Myths and New Realities* (New York: Random House, 1964), 46.

54 "As a tender disciple to mystery": Rick Bass, *The Lost Grizzlies* (Boston: Houghton Mifflin, 1995), 227.

Some Thoughts on Record Production, Its Tools, and Tomorrow's Music Producer

104 This is anecdotal evidence: The earlier the onset of formal musical training, the greater the refinement to the auditory pathway. Changes level off for those beginning their training in their teens. Therefore, brain scientists broadly classify a "musician" as someone who has had five or so years of formal musical training beginning in childhood. See G. Schlaug, "The Brain of Musicians: A Model for Functional and Structural Adaptation," *Annals of the New York Academy of Sciences* 930 (2001): 281–99.

105 "We have critics": Frank Zappa and Peter Occhiogrosso, *The Real Frank Zappa Book* (New York: Simon & Schuster, 1989).

108 In fact, they do not: J. Panksepp and G. Bernatzky, "Emotional Sounds and the Brain: The Neuro-affective Foundations of Musical Appreciation," *Behavioral Processes* 60 (2002): 133–55.

113 It is known that music-induced: P. N. Juslin, and D. Västfjäll, "Emotional Responses to Music: The Need to Consider Underlying Mechanisms," *Behavioral and Brain Sciences* 31 (2008): 559–621.

114 Our self-selected social and physical: P. J. Rentfrow and S. G. Gosling, "The Do Re Mis of Everyday Life: The Structure and Personality Correlates of Music Preferences," *Journal of Personality and Social Psychology*, 84, no. 6 (2003): 1236–56.

118 Long term exposure: J. A. Kaltenbach, "Insights on the Origins of Tinnitus: An Overview of Recent Research," *The Hearing Journal* 62, no. 2 (2009): 26–29.

Modern Recording Fidelity and the Digital Download World

148 "Total album sales": Ben Sisario, "Music Sales Fell in 2008, but Climbed on the Web," *New York Times*, December 31, 2008.

150 The even better news: Apple Computers, "Changes Coming to the iTunes Store," http://www.apple.com/pr/library/2009/01/06itunes.html (January 26, 2009).

Contributors

William Ackerman is known internationally as both the founder of Windham Hill Records and as a guitarist whose work is unusually and compellingly characterized by an emotion-based style of composition and playing. His recordings, and those he has produced, have received numerous Gold and Platinum Record awards. He has performed worldwide in venues as notable as Carnegie Hall, the Kremlin, and the Imperial Palace in Tokyo. Because of the particular success of the Windham Hill approach, Ackerman has lectured at the Harvard, Yale, and Stanford business schools. He won a Grammy for his album *Returning* and works out of his Imaginary Road Studios in Vermont.

Clifford F. Adams teaches courses on the history of rock and roll, and blues and country music, at the University of Cincinnati—College-Conservatory of Music. He holds a degree in music theory and has worked extensively as a keyboardist, guitarist, composer, and producer in Cincinnati, Ohio, for many years.

Kenny Aronoff is justifiably known as one of the world's most influential and in-demand drummers. He first reached a wider public as drummer on ten albums with John Mellencamp and began an extraordinarily energetic career as a session player, touring with artists as diverse as John Fogerty, Jon Bon Jovi, Elton John, Bob Dylan, the Rolling Stones, Vince Gill, Bonnie Raitt, Ray Charles, Trisha Yearwood, Joe Cocker, and innumerable others. He has appeared on literally hundreds of records, thirty of which have been nominated for Grammys. He has performed at the Kennedy Center and in 2009 he played at the Obama Inaugural Celebration Concert at the Lincoln Memorial. Regularly voted #1 Drummer by the readers of *Modern Drummer Magazine*, Aronoff has also been associate professor of percussion at Indiana University.

Adam Ayan is a Grammy, three-time Latin Grammy, and TEC Award–winning mastering engineer at Gateway Mastering Studios in Portland, Maine. His diverse list of credits includes projects for such artists as Madonna, Foo Fighters, Sarah McLachlan, Buckcherry, Pearl Jam, Keith Urban, the Rolling Stones, Nirvana, Rascal Flatts, Carrie Underwood, and Incubus. He has mastered several Grammy Award–winning recordings and has over seventy Gold, Platinum, or Multi-Platinum projects to his credit to date. In addition, he is involved in task forces for the city of

Portland seeking to promote that city's creative economy, founded the nonprofit Portland Music Foundation, and teaches digital audio at the University of Southern Maine's School of Music.

Kevin Becka is the technical editor of *Mix* magazine and an audio instructor who has been director of education at the Conservatory of Recording Arts & Sciences. He has been the editor in chief of *Pro Audio Review* and *Audio Media* (USA), and spent eighteen years in Los Angeles as a recording engineer working with a variety of artists and producers, including Quincy Jones, Kenny G, Michael Bolton, Whitney Houston, and George Benson, among others. He's taught recording as an adjunct professor at Belmont University in Nashville and also at the Rhythmik Music Conservatory in Copenhagen, Denmark.

Rick Clark grew up immersed in music in his hometown of Memphis, Tennessee. Among the many artists with whom he has worked as a musician and producer are Lyle Lovett, Delbert McClinton, John Hiatt, Freddy Fender, Rodney Crowell, and Marty Stuart. As a journalist he has written for *Rolling Stone, Billboard, Mix, Guitar Player,* and others. He is the author of *The Expert's Encyclopedia of Recording* and *Mixing, Recording, and Producing Techniques of the Pros* and produced the first seven volumes of the award-winning

Oxford American Magazine music CDs. In addition, he was music supervisor for Jason Reitman's Oscar-nominated film *Up in the Air* and Billy Bob Thornton's *Jayne Mansfield's Car.* He lives in Santa Monica and Nashville.

David Flitner holds a PhD from Tufts University. He has been a consultant to the US Congress, is the author of two books on American politics, contributed to the *Encyclopedia of the American Presidency*, and written on public affairs and music for numerous publications, from major newspapers to *Billboard.* His primary work is as a composer and musician with the band Thinline.

Bobby Frasier is a guitarist, producer, and audio educator. He has worked as a product specialist for Solid State Logic, Alesis, and Panasonic and is a regular contributor to *Mix.* He teaches professional audio at the Conservatory of Recording Arts and Sciences in Phoenix and performs with the Beatles sound-alike band Marmalade Skies.

Lydia Hutchinson is the founder and was editor and publisher of *Performing Songwriter* magazine, which she started out of her guest bedroom in 1993. She graduated from Louisiana State University with a BA in journalism and advertising, and has lived in Nashville for twenty-five years. She was elected to the Recording Academy's Board of Governors in 2008, is a 2007 graduate of Leadership Music, served as president of the Music Magazine Publisher's Association from 2005 to 2008, is a member of NAMM, and is on the faculty of Songwriter101.com. She now edits performingsongwriter.com.

Bob Ludwig, Grammy and Latin Grammy–winning mastering engineer, holds a bachelor of music degree in music education and a master of music degree in trumpet and music literature from the Eastman School of Music. While at Eastman he also played principal trumpet with the Utica Symphony Orchestra. He is president and owner of Gateway Mastering Studios in Portland, Maine. Ludwig has mastered countless Gold and Platinum records. He was the first person to be honored with the Les Paul Award for "consistently outstanding achievements in the professional audio industry." He has won fifteen TEC Awards for "Outstanding Creative Achievement, Mastering Engineer." Gateway Mastering Studios has won the TEC Award eleven times. Allmusic.com presently lists forty-three pages of credits for Ludwig, possibly more than any engineer. Special articles on Ludwig and Gateway Mastering have appeared in the *New York Times*, the *Boston Globe, USA Today*, the *Portland Press Herald*, and the Associated Press. A Fellow of the Audio Engineering Society and a past chairman of the NY Section, he was recently cochairman of the six-thousand-plus member Producers & Engineers Wing of the Recording Academy.

Cookie Marenco has engineered or produced five Grammy-nominated records, several Gold Records, and an Academy Award–winning documentary. She has worked with artists as diverse as Max Roach, Brain, Tony Furtado, Charlie Haden, Tony Levin, Mary Chapin Carpenter, and Turtle Island String Quartet, and on projects for the Monterey Jazz Festival, Telluride Bluegrass Festival, Marinfest, Hard Rock Café, Windham Hill Records, Verve, Rounder Records, Sony, Warner Bros., and others. She was the first woman to sit on the Grammy panel judging surround sound. As owner of OTR Studios in California's Bay Area, she concentrates on ultra-high-end audio authenticity; and as founder of Blue Coast Records, she has done groundbreaking work with the creation of audio files called 9624, which are twenty times the size of MP3s. She launched DownloadsNOW! for the delivery of music via Direct Stream Digital, the first company to do so worldwide. Marenco is a frequent speaker at university audio programs.

Rob Reinhart started his professional broadcasting career while still in high school, working the campus radio station at the University of Michigan in his hometown of Ann Arbor. He earned a degree in psychology from the

University of Michigan. He has owned a small ad agency and radio production company; written, produced and acted in syndicated comedy for radio through Olympia, Premier, and the ABC Comedy Network; voiced thousands of radio and TV commercials for clients including Kmart, Walmart, and the Democratic National Committee; raised funds for many public radio stations; and consulted on numerous media projects. In 1995 he launched *Acoustic Café*, an independent, syndicated music program heard on eighty-five commercial and noncommercial stations across the United States and worldwide via Voice of America. The show features appearances and interviews with a wide range of singer-songwriters from Willie Nelson, Lyle Lovett, and Norah Jones to Beck, Ani DiFranco, and Joan Baez. *Acoustic Café* may be heard at acafe.com. Reinhart lives in Ann Arbor with his family and a golden retriever, Fibber, named for a classic radio show.

Gino Robair has created music for dance, theater, television, silent film, and gamelan orchestra, and his works have been performed throughout North America, Europe, and Japan. As a percussionist, he has recorded with Tom Waits, Anthony Braxton, Terry Riley, and Fred Frith. Robair spent five years as composer in residence with the California Shakespeare Festival and served as music director for the CBS animated series *The Twisted Tales of Felix the Cat*. His commercial work includes themes for the MTV and Comedy Central cable networks. As a writer about music technology, Robair has contributed to *Mix*, *Remix*, *Keyboard*, *Guitar Player*, and *Electronic Musician* magazine, where he was an editor for eleven years. In addition, he has authored two books, including *The Ultimate Personal Recording Studio* (Thompson, 2006).

Eugene S. Robinson is, by his own admission, a polymath. His work ranges from movies and television to journalism and rock performance. His articles have appeared in publications such as *GQ*, *The Wire*, *Art Forum*, *LA Weekly*, *Decibel*, and many others. He is the former editor in chief of *EQ* magazine, and is the author of *Fight* and a novel, *A Long Slow Screw*. In addition, he is singer for the rock band Oxbow.

Susan Rogers earned her PhD in cognitive psychology from McGill University in Montreal. Prior to academic life, in a career spanning over twenty years, she produced, engineered, and/or mixed albums for Prince, David Byrne, Barenaked Ladies, Geggy Tah, Tricky, the Jacksons, Jeff Black, Robben Ford, Michael Penn, Rusted Root, and many more, earning dozens of Gold and Platinum albums as well as the distinction of being one of a handful of women who succeeded as a record producer/engineer in a profoundly male-dominated field. She is currently an associate professor at Berklee College of Music in Boston, teaching music production, audio electronics, music cognition, and psychoacoustics, and is the director of the Berklee Music Perception and Cognition Lab for Auditory Research. In her own words, her career highlights include "being told by Miles Davis that even though I didn't play an instrument I was indeed a musician because, as he put it, some of the best musicians he knew weren't musicians. Finally understanding what he meant."